Learning to Pray

Learning to PRAY

HOWARD W. ROBERTS

BROADMAN PRESS
Nashville, Tennessee

Unless otherwise indicated, Scripture quotations are from the Revised
Standard Version of the Bible, copyrighted 1946, 1952, © 1971, 1973.

Library of Congress Cataloging in Publication Data

Roberts, Howard W., 1947-
  Learning to pray.

  1. Prayer.   I. Title.
BV210.2.R586   1984   248.3'2   82-74296
ISBN 0-8054-5195-1 (pbk.)

For my children—

Father,

Your other name is Surprise! I hear you and see you in the faces and voices of my children. One of the great joys in life is for me to call home and hear one of the children answer. As soon as my voice is recognized, there is a radiance of sheer delight in the voice that says, "Hi, Dad!" I'm taken aback every time by how excited Melanie, Danita, or Brandon is to talk to me. I'm glad for that. I am astounded how such a small exchange makes such a large contribution to my joy.

It makes me want to take off my shoes. For Moses it was the burning bush. For Isaiah it was worship in the Temple. For me, with the aid of Ma Bell, it's a child's voice that speaks unadulterated love, acceptance, and joy that causes me to know I am standing on holy ground. Thanks for the surprise. What is even more surprising is that even when I anticipate being surprised, I am still surprised. Your other name has to be Surprise! Amen.

Acknowledgments

I am indebted to several people for their assistance in the publication of this book. To Sandra Gardner, friend and secretary, who said, "What people need is a book of prayers to help them when they are sick and when they are dying." Her suggestion encouraged me to begin this venture. Her typing and retyping enabled me to complete this project. To Jerry and Susan Cauley, colleagues in ministry, who have dreamed with me and for me about publishing a book. To Peggy Roberts, my wife and friend, who always was eager to listen with interest to what I had been writing. To people to whom I have been a pastor who have been willing to share their needs and thus have contributed to my learning to pray. I want to thank the following for allowing me to use prayers that dealt with crises in their lives: Delores Brown, Emajean, and Leonard Lane.

These people belong to the order of Barnabas. They have been encouragers to me. They have believed in me. For them, I am grateful.

Introduction

Every person has a god—that to which he attributes ultimate worth. Thus worship is the worth-ship one gives to his god. Prayer is the vehicle that a person uses to commune with his god.

This book is written from the Christian perspective, and I understand the God I worship to be the Creator, Redeemer, and Sustainer of the universe. A person's view of God and self-esteem are interrelated in the ability to pray.

Praying seldom is easy. It isn't easy for a number of reasons. Some expect prayer to change things. When it does not, they quit praying, at least to that god. Some use prayer to deny reality, and for them it is an escape. For others, prayer is a means to manipulate life; prayer and magic become synonymous for these people. There are those for whom prayer is the deep calling the deep. Out of the depth and struggle of their lives, they seek connection with the One who will listen to their yearnings and journey with them in their struggles.

Prayer is revealing. It tells what we think of God and of ourselves. Prayer demonstrates how we view life and what we think life's possibilities are. Prayer can be an avenue of personal growth. The title of this book, *Learning to Pray,* is chosen purposefully. I am constantly in the process of learning to pray. I will never arrive at the point where I say, "I know how to pray." Constantly present in all my prayers is the prayer, "Lord, teach me to pray."

This book is telescopic in design. I begin by struggling with what prayer is and what prayer does. I share some of my struggles and difficulties about prayer. Then I point out that usually we begin praying for ourselves and soon discover that prayer has social dimensions. As one prays, the circle of people for whom one prays enlarges and expands to include friends and enemies, the sick, the grievers, the church, and the world.

Most of the names of persons in the situations described and in the prayers have been changed. This is due to the personal and confidential nature of the material.

The purpose of this book is to help us in our pilgrimages. We are in the process of learning to pray; in our individual lives, we are asking, "Lord, teach us to pray." I hope through this book that God will be teaching us to pray and that we will be eager learners.

Contents

1

Learning to Pray

He was praying in a certain place, and when he ceased, one of his disciples said to him, "Lord, teach us to pray, as John taught his disciples." And he said to them, "When you pray, say 'Father, hallowed be thy name. Thy kingdom come. Give us each day our daily bread; and forgive us our sins, for we ourselves forgive every one who is indebted to us; and lead us not into temptation' " (Luke 11:1-4).

The first day of class a fellow student asked Professor Wayne Oates, "How do I learn to be a pastor?"

Oates immediately answered, "Be one!" He went on to explain that he had no bag of tricks to hand our pastoral care class that would make us pastors. Rather, as we ministered to people, examined and evaluated what we did, and dialogued with colleagues and supervisors, we would learn to be pastors.

Jesus' disciples asked, "How do we learn to pray?" Jesus answered, "Pray." He offered the Disciples' Prayer (often called the Lord's Prayer) as a model of what prayer is and what prayer does.

What Prayer Is

Prayer crises have been common in my life. The first crisis occurred as a teenager when I wondered, *Why am I praying? Is anyone listening? If God is listening, why doesn't he do something?* Numerous times since adolescence I have concluded that my prayers were getting no higher than the proverbial ceiling. These crises in prayer have been pivotal points in my struggle with prayer, causing me to wonder what prayer is and who is listening to the prayers I offer.

Prayer is communion with God. It involves verbal and nonverbal expressions and telling and listening by the one praying. Prayer is trilogical because it involves God listening to my best self and my worst self talk to each other. William James, a well-known psychologist of religion, understood prayer as an interchange of ideas and feelings which he identified as intercourse with the Ideal Companion. In the first word of the Disciples' Prayer, Jesus disclosed to whom prayer is to be addressed. He said, "Father." Judaism already knew God as Father, but the direct, warm, personal, childlike address, "Abba," was new. It was almost like our word *dad,* implying close, intimate, day-to-day encounters between parent and child. Prayer is communication between God and me on the most intimate level of relationship.

Prayer understood thus becomes communication between friends. Friendships do not develop by two people nodding to each other occasionally. On first meeting, persons may appear aloof. Then, as mutual events are experienced and joys and sorrows are shared, empathy develops, bonding occurs, and friends are as one. A friendship is established that can last a lifetime. So it is with friendship beyond time. Prayer is the communication system of this friendship. Prayer becomes an experience of pure love and trust leading to self-disclosure; as a result, I discover myself to be at one with God. Paul implied this type of relationship when he wrote to the Corinthians that, even when there was trouble on every hand, he was not without a friend.

I feel in conflict with God when I perceive my words and actions have not communicated love, justice, and mercy. Part of my communicating with God is putting myself in his place and attempting to see my life as he sees it. Such an approach enables me to tell God anything because I admit that he already knows it. I feel at one with God when I express my joys and agonies and feel that God has listened, that what is happening to me matters to him. This happens most often when I express my deep frustrations and aggravations about my job or my family. Often these expressions take no verbal forms but are groanings directed toward God.

Thus, words are not essential for this oneness to occur. As the hymn writer suggests, "Prayer is the soul's sincere desire, Unuttered or expressed." On October 3, 1972 I stood in a hospital corridor gazing through a glass into a face I had never seen before. My prayer took the shape of teardrops rolling down my cheeks. There was Melanie. No word could say what I felt, but my tears thanked God for the gift of life in the form of a daughter. I was communing and communicating with God.

Barriers to Prayer

We are relational creatures by nature and by need. As created beings we have the capacity to relate to other human beings and to God. As Jesus suggested in the parable of the prodigal son, we are not our authentic selves apart from God. A crisis occurs in prayer when prayer becomes meaningless. When this happens, I am in the far country and there are many barriers to my communing with God that include low self-esteem, anger, fear, and guilt.

Low Self-Esteem. As a youth I suffered from a superiority complex. Others saw me as self-assured, confident, cocky, and conceited. Actually, I was shaky and frightened. I overcompensated for inferior feelings by acting superior. I did not consider myself worth much and doubted that anyone would like me. Thomas Merton once said that there is only one thing a person desires more than happiness and that is approval. I had an insatiable appetite for approval which I thought would say I was somebody. But I discovered that receiving approval was like drinking salt water—the more I received, the more I needed to quench my thirst. It was natural for me to transfer my perceptions about authority figures and their expectations onto God, the ultimate authority figure.

Where I grew up, the beatitude of reality was, "Blessed are they who work hard, for they shall earn acceptance and approval." I became trapped into doing rather than being. Prayer at that juncture was static monologue: "Lord, tell me what you want me to do." When I listened for a response, all I perceived was, "Don't do anything that anybody won't like!" I felt worthless, and prayer became meaningless. I continued my perfunctory religious rituals, including praying. Although prayer was meaningless, I wouldn't admit it, and I continued saying my prayers because I needed God's approval.

I was helped over the prayer barrier of low self-esteem when someone suggested that Jesus said we had to love ourselves in order to love others. I knew I was supposed to love God and everybody else, but

I thought I was supposed to hate myself. My concept of prayer began to change as I discovered there was a correlation between my love for God, my love for others, and how I felt about myself.

Some young people are fond of saying, "God made me and he don't make no junk." It was a struggle for me to become aware that I had worth just because God created me. This awareness has resulted in prayer becoming a dynamic dialogue. Because I am of worth, created by God, what happens to me matters to him. I can tell him how I feel without fear of reprisal or rejection, as in this prayer:

> God,
>
> I don't want to be here today. I have every reason to like it here, but the pit of my stomach is a churning bundle of anxiety. All the outward signs point toward happiness and success. Have I become secure in this place? Is it now time to move to another place? Or am I really insecure here and hope to find security somewhere else?
>
> What shall I do? I'm unhappy but I don't know why. My motivation is gone. I don't want to work here anymore. Amen.

Feelings of low self-esteem continue to surface periodically. When they do, the prayer barrier goes up. Failure to express the feelings results in prayer reverting to a meaningless static monologue.

Anger. Anger is a barrier to prayer. Where I grew up, anger was equated with sin. I learned early that I was not supposed to get angry. When I became angry, I coped by denying it. I still remember the relief I felt the day I stumbled over Ephesians 4:26-27, "Be angry but do not sin; do not let the sun go down on your anger, and give no opportunity to the devil." Anger is a feeling—it is neither right nor wrong. Anger is part of my natural warning system that helps me identify a potential problem. I need to get at the root of the problem and seek to dissolve my anger appropriately.

A woman, who was angry at God because life had not gone well for her, recently said to her son who was anticipating surgery, "I would pray for you if I believed in prayer anymore." She believed God should have worked out things better for her. She was angry at God, and the barrier kept her from communicating with him. Her prayer crisis was caused by the barrier of anger.

An approach often taken with anger is to turn it inward, resulting in depression. When this is done, Frederick Buechner, in *Wishful Thinking,* suggests that it is a "feast fit for a king." The chief drawback with such a feast is that what I am wolfing down is me. The anger turned in on myself remains a barrier to prayer.

Job expressed his anger to God several times. Here is one example:

> As for me, is my complaint against man?
>   Why should I not be impatient?
> Look at me, and be appalled,
>   and lay your hand upon your mouth.
> When I think of it I am dismayed,
>   and shuddering seizes my flesh (Job 21:4-6).

Job discovered that God was big enough to receive his anger and not destroy him. Making this discovery for myself has aided me in dealing constructively with the strong emotion of anger. I need to tell God my feelings even though I know he knows what they are. If I am detained because my wife, Peggy, is late, I become angry. She knows I am angry and why. I know I am angry and why. The wall of tension, however, continues to separate us until we verbalize our feelings to each other and dissolve the anger. The same is true when I am angry at God. My telling him is part of the process necessary to tear down this prayer barrier.

Fear. Intimate relationship with God involves self-disclosure, which is threatening. A barrier to self-disclosure is fear, and risk is the flip side of fear. A person fears disclosing himself because to disclose himself is to risk rejection. Bruce Larson, a minister-writer, spent a sabbatical leave talking to psychologists from all over the world. He asked each of them to sum up in one word what promotes mental health and prevents mental illness. The ability to take risks was the answer he received most often.

I often encounter people who are hurting in their relationships with others. The barrier most often erected in these relationships is fear. When asked why they don't communicate openly and directly with the ones with whom there is conflict, they respond, "I'm afraid"; "I'm afraid of what she'll say"; "I'm afraid I'll explode."

Fear often blocks my communication with God. My fear of rejection by God keeps me from stating my innermost thoughts and desires. Fear controls me in spite of my intellectual awareness that God already knows my thoughts and feelings. "How could he love me if I told him what I really think?" is the bottom line of my fear.

Jacob's fear controlled him. For twenty years Jacob ran scared. Although he said his prayers during those twenty years, he was not really at one with God until that night by the Jabbok River when he wrestled all night long. Realizing that he could no longer hide, he named his fears to himself and to God. The wall came down, Jacob passed through one of his prayer crises, and his whole identity was changed. Jacob became Israel.

Guilt. A person's emotional reaction to having done something wrong is guilt. Guilt does its damage because the guilty person tries to deal with his guilt alone, which is about as easy as sitting on one's own lap.

The biblical word for wrongdoing is *sin.* While sin may be against another person, it always is against God. When we sin, we feel guilt. Guilt is a barrier to prayer. It causes us to feel separated from God and unable to be our true selves until we invite God to manage our guilt through forgiveness. Then, at least for a moment, the vicious circle stops and we can stand on solid ground.

Guilt blocked communication with God for Judas, who attempted to deal with his guilt alone. He sought relief from his guilt by returning the money he had received. When that didn't work, Judas was overcome with despair, becoming so confused that he was blind to any presence other than his own. Judas saw no solution other than his and conceived of no absolution beyond himself. Judas had himself on his hands. He tied the rope around his neck and kicked away the stool, trying alone to get himself off his hands. Guilt was a barrier to prayer for Judas.

Low self-esteem, anger, fear, and guilt are four barriers to prayer. There are others. These may occur separately or in a variety of combinations. They declare prayer null and void and create a prayer crisis. With God's help in identifying these barriers, they can come down and we can commune with God as friend with friend. This is prayer.

What Prayer Does

A clear demarcation between what prayer is and what prayer does cannot be maintained. As one communes with God (what prayer is), the barriers to prayer dissipate (part of what prayer does). Prayer does at least four things: (1) it respects God, (2) it expects his kingdom, (3) it benefits the one praying, and (4) it affects persons and situations for which one intercedes. Part of what prayer does is explainable and comprehensible. There also is a part of what prayer does that remains a mystery. Just believing that we can communicate with God is mystical. We must leave room for mystery in prayer. I agree with Paul that "we do not know how to pray as we ought, but the Spirit himself intercedes for us with sighs too deep for words" (Rom. 8:26).

Respects God. The first thing prayer does is express reverence for God. Respect for God, however, has fallen on hard times because in developing reasoning skills we have neglected intuitive powers. This neglect has contributed to the idolatrous expression in American culture that we are self-made people. Having accepted the Protestant work ethic as our salvation, we have tied our worth to what we do. We conclude that the more we do, the more we are worth. Often we think Jesus' words, "Hallowed be [your] name," refer to ourselves rather than to God.

Having concluded erroneously that we have made ourselves by the sweat of our brows, we are skeptical about what prayer does. Our skepticism results either from our conclusion that God is impotent or from our uncertainty of his existence. God often seems far off at best and absent at worst. Respect for him at such times may be impossible. People's skepticism about God and their conviction that he is powerless are expressed by a state of boredom with existence. People conclude that if God is the basis of meaningful living and if life is boring for them, then God must not exist or he is ineffective.

Being bored with life may suggest that we see luxuries as necessities. Life as we view it has become like many cereals; we refuse to taste it unless it is sugar coated. My ten-year-old daughter already may be afflicted with boredom, as reflected in her language. Recently she said, "Ice cream is boring." That made no sense to me because she often adds ice cream to the grocery list. I asked for interpretation and she gladly responded, "Ice cream by itself is boring—you know, without strawberries and milk to make a milkshake." Do we not feel that the extras are essential for an exciting life? Since mere being is boring, God must be out of life, nonexistent, or at least uninvolved and ineffective. If God doesn't sweeten life our way, then we give him no respect.

Skepticism about prayer also results from our technological advances which have convinced us that given enough time, human beings can do anything. Part of this is because of our transition to the city, where we may marvel at all the wonders of mankind and be blind to the greater wonders God has created.

I am an inland creature, born and bred in Kentucky. However, I have a fascination for the ocean. Each year on my annual pilgrimage to the beach, I am amazed how the mixture of sand, sky, salt water, and sea breeze can cleanse my being. On at least one occasion whenever I am at the beach, I position myself so that all I can see is sand, ocean, and sky—nothing man-made in sight or sound. I become engulfed, awed, and, as Sidney Lanier said, I "build me a nest on the greatness of God."

The destructiveness of which we are now capable contributes to skepticism about what prayer does. Many teenagers are pessimistic about the future, frightened by the possibility of a nuclear holocaust. Not only can we destroy our generation, but future generations. "Where is God in all of this?" is a frequent question.

To honor God requires that we believe in him. The church has not been exempt from skepticism. Our worship often reveals that we believe more in ourselves than we believe in God. Theodore W. Jennings, Jr., suggests that people learn to be atheists, not from too much contact with the world, but from too much contact with the church. In praying, the primary emphasis is to be upon God rather than upon ourselves or our needs. To respect God means that his reputation is at stake in us. Respect for God can help our daily desire to be:

Father,
    Enable me to bring honor to you. Protect me from tarnishing

the beauty of your grace and from cooling the warmth of your love. Amen.

Prayer honors God.

Expects the Kingdom. Jesus' life portrayed a new kind of era, bounded at its beginning and ending by decisive expressions of divine love. God's kingdom was never intended to be a political entity with a geographical location. The kingdom of God has to do with each of us. For us to pray for God's kingdom to come means that we are requesting and desiring some changes in ourselves. That involves struggle and hard work. Often we would prefer God's kingdom to go, rather than to come. We need God's help to open us to desire his kingdom to come in us. To commune with God may result in this desire.

Benefits the One Praying. Empirical evidence is available to support the statement that prayer can benefit the one praying. Blood pressure may decline, heart and respiratory rates may decrease, and anxiety level may reduce for the one praying. Practically everyone who ever prayed offers the subjective testimony that he felt better afterward. Prayer positively affects a person's attitudes and actions. One example is John Woolman, who through prayer became convicted of the wrongness of being a slave owner. Not only did he become convinced himself but he also persuaded all Quakers to arrive at the same conclusion. By 1787 no Quakers owned slaves.

What happened to John Woolman indicates that prayer changes attitudes and life-styles. My first awareness of this happened seren-dipitously during my daily swim. I had been wrestling with a sermon idea that would not give me its name or reveal its shape. After a few laps of swimming, the sermon idea began to roll through my mind. As I continued to swim, the shape and name of the sermon surfaced. Soon after this experience, I noticed that much of my swim time was being used to struggle with personal and professional issues. Praying involves identifying feelings such as anger, guilt, low self-esteem, and fear, and calls for me to wrestle with these in communion with God.

I often sense the presence of God very keenly while swimming and experience myself in dialogue with him as I swim. I experience activity and communion with God simultaneously. I think this is what Brother

Lawrence, a Carmelite lay brother, means when he talks about prayer as practicing the presence of God. Because I cannot talk while I swim, I commune with God in silence and am developing the capacity to listen to God and communicate with him in the silence. I am convinced that the Spirit pleads for me when I am in over my head and cannot form the words. Prayer affects me positively.

Benefits Others. Prayer is mystery. No one knows all that prayer does. Part of a mechanistic view of the universe concludes that everything functions in a predictable fashion. If everything is predictable, prayer can affect nothing beyond the one praying. However, if all creation is in process, as Paul suggested in Romans 8:18-25 and to which Chardin, a Jesuit priest and paleontologist, gives strong supportive evidence, then prayer can affect life beyond the one praying.

It is impossible to know all the factors involved, including the freedom of the universe and human freedom, that God considers in caring for a person. Yet, for this very reason we need to put at his disposal our every resource. To pray for another person really means to let his needs become ours. To plead for the needs of another is genuine when I am willing to give a part of my energy to God for his use in caring for that person. Glenn Hinson, in *The Reaffirmation of Prayer,* identifies this as "love energy." Because God has limited himself by creating us as free beings, there may be some things he cannot do. But we can add our love energies to his to benefit others. Healing is just one example. Much more healing occurs now than in the first century—a result of humanity's ability to learn, a gift from God.

God is working with us in our freedom to join him in bringing healing, help, and hope to others as he draws all of his creation to himself. Who would have believed that millions of people of diverse cultural, religious, and national backgrounds would be calling for a freeze on nuclear weapons? This call began in the church, and prayer seems to have affected this concern positively as the call has bubbled up in the church and now is flowing out into the world. Prayer affects others.

Prayer crises are common to us. Often they are frightening; they are always disturbing. These crises cause us to examine again what prayer is and what prayer does. We must struggle with these questions in learning to pray. As prayer crises arise, they are pivotal points which can take us into deeper dialogue with God. Learning to pray is a lifelong process through which we learn about God and ourselves.

I will never arrive at the conclusive conviction, "I know how to pray." Rather, I will continue to say, "I am praying, Lord. Teach me to pray."

Note

1. Theodore W. Jennings, Jr., "Prayer: The Call for God," *The Christian Century,* April 15, 1981, p. 414.

2

Learning to Pray for Ourselves

And I tell you, Ask and it will be given you; seek, and you will find; knock, and it will be opened to you. For every one who asks, receives, and he who seeks, finds, and to him who knocks it will be opened (Luke 11:9-10).

Learning to pray for ourselves is a natural step to take after examining what prayer is and what it does. As we learn to pray for ourselves, we discover that our needs, concerns, and struggles are common to all people. Prayer then becomes a social expression, as demonstrated in the Disciples' Prayer: "Give us . . . forgive us . . . lead us not. . . ." Elton Trueblood's suggestion that a person soak himself in the Disciples' Prayer and then pray freely is a helpful one.[1]

Daily Needs

Jesus suggested that the order of our priorities is to be respect for God, desire for his kingdom to come, and daily needs. Now let us focus on our daily needs of food, forgiveness, and deliverance, acknowledging that God is the Creator and Sustainer of all life.

Food. When Jesus referred to daily bread, no doubt he recalled the history of his people in the wilderness when manna was their daily food. There was enough manna for each day, but any attempt to take more than the daily need resulted in spoilage. Who of us has not been guilty of taking more than we needed? Look at our nation. We are 6 percent of the world's population consuming 35 percent of the world's goods. We have become "thingmatized," and our living spoils. Ghandi was right in saying that there is enough for everyone's need but not enough for everyone's greed. We attempt to fill time by filling our stomachs. Raiding the refrigerator as a cure for spiritual malnutrition is gluttony. We need to come back to the simple but not simplistic prayer, "Give us each day our daily bread. Help us to want only the amount of food we need for today." We need to experience the miracle of sufficiency and live more simply so that others may simply live.

Peggy and I married thirteen years ago. Pizza was a weekly meal, and the two of us ate the whole thing. Now there are five of us, and pizza is still a favorite family meal. The same pizza pan now holds enough for five instead of two. We are learning about the miracle of sufficiency. To communicate daily with God about what we need will help our learning. It also will aid in relieving guilt, one of the barriers to prayer. This prayer about daily needs brings these issues to God:

Father,
The scales tell me what you've been telling me for a long time. Daily I consume more than I need. I have this "wanting" compulsion. I am slowly realizing that when I take more than I need I am taking from someone else. I need your help in fixing my "wanters" so that I may experience the miracle of your sufficiency fully and become part of the solution to the daily needs of others, rather than part of the problem as I have been in the past. Amen.

Forgiveness. Once our physical needs are cared for, we can become concerned about our spiritual and emotional well-being. We need the daily renewal which comes through forgiveness of sins. Was not Jesus saying in the Disciples' Prayer that a person cannot live by bread alone? One must have forgiveness. Many of us could live healthily longer without food than without forgiveness.

Sin means to do wrong; to be concerned only for myself with no consideration for the needs of others. Sin is craziness. Jesus said the prodigal came to his senses when he confessed, "Father, I have sinned against heaven and before you" (Luke 15:21). God is the one who can deal properly with our sins, and daily we need to confess our sins to him. Here is an individual confessional prayer:

O Father,
Sin scorches my life and makes it barren. I know that your forgiveness is the only oasis for my parched life.

Hear my confession.

I have done wrong and blamed it on another.

Forgive me.

I have benefited from the hurt of another and enjoyed it.

Forgive me.

I have passed on information that was confidential.

Forgive me.

I have refused to look into the eyes of the hungry.

Forgive me.

I have resisted taking the hand of the lonely.

Forgive me.

I have refused to touch the sick.

Forgive me.

I have avoided the bereaved and dying.

Forgive me.

Cleanse me, Father. Make me whole again so that I may live—live for you. Amen.

Not only as individuals have we sinned but also we have joined others in wrongdoing. Often it is through daily confessional prayers that we may become aware of how we have teamed up with others to do wrong. Is this not what Jesus had in mind when he suggested that his disciples pray, "Forgive us . . . "? Our collective sins include overconsumption, prejudice, and revenge, to name only three. Daily we need to come to our senses by confessing our collective sins, as in this prayer:

Our Father,

We have contaminated our lives with sins and stunted the growth you offered us. We confess our sins to you. Hear our pleas. Forgive us for our sins as we forgive those who sin against us.

We have not just disagreed with one another. We have been mean and vindictive in our attitudes toward others. Forgive us, Father, for our mean-spiritedness and our vindictiveness.

We have been so determined to take care of ourselves that we have taken from others. Forgive us, Father, for our greed.

We have looked and listened to others. When their skin color and accent were different from ours, we put them in what we perceived to be their places. Forgive us, Father, for our prejudices.

Father, we need to be cleansed by your forgiveness in order to grow toward maturity. Only with clean hands and pure hearts created by your forgiving love are we able to begin seriously writing your love in our lives and conveying it to others. Help us, Father, with this ultimate responsibility. Amen.

Jesus suggested that the ability to experience forgiveness is related directly to the willingness to forgive. Here is where I stumble. Sometimes I want to harbor grudges or hang onto resentments because I have been wronged and feel that the one who has wronged me must pay by feeling the heat of my resentment. Part of my resentment may be that I have forgiven the same person on other occasions for the same wrong. Jesus questioned whether forgiveness had occurred if a person found it necessary to keep score. I wonder if God ever thinks about me like I think about others. If he did, he might say:

I'm tired of forgiving Howard Roberts. When I do forgive him and think he is on the way to getting his life in order, he turns right around and sins again. I've forgiven him 25,363 times. That's enough! I've been a very patient God!

We experience forgiveness in proportion to our willingness to forgive. Daily we need to be forgiven and forgiving.

Deliverance. Daily we need to be delivered. In Luke 11:4 Jesus said, "Lead us not into temptation." Matthew 6:13 adds the parallel statement, "Deliver us from evil." This petition troubles me. Is God leading us into temptation? Is he testing us to determine the strength of our moral fiber? Is God a heavenly psychologist who has designed the human experiment to measure how people respond to the options before them and why? If the answer is yes, we don't need a "friend" like this.

Jesus, in his wilderness temptation experiences, in his ministry, and on the cross, demonstrated that God was neither tempting him nor testing him to determine his strengths and weaknesses. Rather, Jesus says that temptation comes with the human territory as a person searches out limitations. We may attempt to be more or less than the human beings we were created to be. To go either way is sin.

James later wrote a very clear and unprecedented statement about the nature of God which is found no other place in the Bible:

> Let no one say when he is tempted, "I am tempted by God"; for God cannot be tempted with evil and he himself tempts no one; but each person is tempted when he is lured and enticed by his own desire (Jas. 1:13-14).

In speaking of temptation, Jesus was referring to the fierce hardships inherent in living in this world. The request is that people who are hard-pressed may be saved from tests too difficult for them, just as they may be saved from debilitating hunger. Jesus emphasized that hard times will come. What we need every day is the strength to face difficult times and to be guided away from doing evil.

God is our Deliverer. Deliverance from the biblical perspective does not infer that God is a "body snatcher" rushing in and yanking us out of a burning building like a fireman in a rescue operation. Rather, deliverance is more like the work of an obstetrician or midwife at the birth of a child. I was part of the delivery team at the births of Danita and Brandon. The nurses, doctors, and I went with Peggy through the two birth processes. We journeyed through those experiences together.

Every day has the potential for difficult times. I need to rely on God to guide me through those times so that, when confronted with difficult decisions, I will not give in to evil. "Lead us not into temptation" is a negative way of saying, "Deliver us from evil." Whether stated positively or negatively, or both, one of my daily needs is to be guided away from doing evil. Here is a prayer I have offered for deliverance:

> Father,
>   Help me to sense your constant presence with me today. When difficulties arise, deliver me from giving in to evil. Deliver me from the evil of responding in kind to those who do harm to me. Help me to turn the other cheek. Keep far from me the desire to bring

down, to harm, or to destroy another person. Deliver me from degrading those who out of fear for themselves do not remain as loyal as they had promised. Deliver me from the evil of selling the principles by which I have lived and the commitment I have promised for a bowl of security or a dish of approval. Deliver me from the evil of condemning another person because of the hurt I experience. Deliver me from the evil of retaliation. When I am taunted by the temptation to do something to prove my worth, deliver me from the evil of overdoing and overworking.

Father, make me conscious of the daily option not to do evil, and assure me of your guidance in delivering me away from doing evil.

I offer this prayer in the name of the one who teaches me to pray, Jesus Christ, the Lord. Amen.

A Pilgrimage of Prayer

Learning to pray is best accomplished by praying. The most important thing Jesus said about prayer is to keep at it. This requires discipline. The verses of Scripture at the beginning of the chapter were taken out of the context of two illustrations Jesus used to emphasize prayer persistence to his disciples. A cursory reading of Luke 11:1-13, as well as the parable of the unjust judge, has lent to the snappy decision that if we pester God long enough and badger him long enough he finally will give us what we want. Ask, seek, knock has been interpreted as God saying, "Your wish is my command." This may be a cute statement by a romanticist, but as a description of God, it makes him a heavenly bellhop who is at our disposal to do our bidding. Persistent praying is not wringing gifts from an unwilling God.

Persistence in prayer really is an act of faith. It is a testimony to our belief in a loving, personal God. We are going to One who knows our needs better than we know them ourselves and whose heart toward us is one of generous love.

I am confident that God answers every prayer, and I do not mean with a trite yes, no, maybe, or later. Rather, God answers every prayer by listening. That is a response. Frustration springs up in me when I am in a conversation with a person and I see his *eyes* wander. What has distracted him? Is he disinterested in me? Is he bored with what I am saying? I know he isn't listening. I may stop talking and he doesn't even notice! Jesus said this will never happen with prayer. "When you pray," he said, "ask [and you will receive a hearing], seek [and you will find a listening Friend], knock [and the door of receptiveness will be opened to you]."

When I arrive home from a very frustrating pastoral experience and begin telling Peggy about it, I don't want any suggestions about how I could have handled the situation better. Nor do I want comments about what a rotten so-and-so some person is. I want Peggy to listen. Jesus said we can be assured of God's receptiveness to our prayers.

As a pastor, I have had to keep at prayer. There always are the sick who want me to pray with them and for them. Often I am with the dying who want me to pray. Every week there is the demand of prayers for worship. Wanting my prayers to be neither empty phrases nor vain repetitions, I have had to keep at prayer. My interest and need for prayer have caused me to reflect on my prayer pilgrimage which reveals partially how praying has developed for me. I have discovered that my prayers are affected by the image I have of God. Thus my prayer pilgrimage reveals a developing view of God.

Santa Claus. My earliest visual image of God was that of a grand, old, white-bearded man. Although he did not wear a red suit or have a cottony white beard, the similarity to Santa Claus is clear. Perhaps the correlation of God with Santa Claus partially resulted from the mixing of the "sellabration" and the celebration of Christmas. The similarity was reflected not only in my visual image but also in the word formations of my prayers. Long after my belief in Santa Claus had changed, my concept of God continued to have a Santa taint. This concept continued into my early school years, and those prayers were filled with magic and fantasy. Somewhere, probably at church and at home, I had learned that I should just ask God for whatever I wanted because he could do anything. I wanted a train set, and the substance of my prayers was, "God, I want a new electric train." After several days passed and God did not deliver, I prayed, "God, *please* give me a new electric train." Still, no train. I suggested, "God, since you can do anything, why don't you just make me a train? If you make it, it won't be like any other train anybody has ever seen." What an opportunity for God! Here was his chance to prove to me and everyone I knew what a great train builder he was. Much later I did receive an electric train, but I didn't think God had anything to do with my receiving it. I had concluded that God wasn't into giving trains to little kids.

Angry Old Man. As I grew in stature and wisdom, I also grew in fear of God. I began to perceive God demanding his "pound of flesh," as Shakespeare put it. The beard on God's face now became over-shadowed by his scowl of anger. If he could do anything, he certainly could destroy me, and I was afraid he would. I was a sinner in the hands of an angry God. What must I do? I must do something to make him neutral. God seemed so angry that I doubted I had the capacity to make him happy, but I hoped I could make him unangry. I began to work my magic to combat God's anger. I developed a compulsion to pray every day, usually lying in bed in the darkness of the night before I dozed off to sleep. On several occasions, I awoke with the jolt of awareness that I had forgotten to "say my prayers." I was glad God had let me live but more frightened than ever, thinking I had made him angrier at me. The content of those prayers, as I recall, was evidence that I was saying prayers rather than praying. "God, please forgive me for forgetting to pray today. Help me to be a better person. Forgive me for all the sins I have committed today, even the ones I didn't know I did. Amen." Such phrases now seem like a version of "Now I lay me down to sleep . . . should I die before I wake, I pray the Lord my soul will take." Jesus said we should not use empty phrases or vain repetitions. Learning to pray is a process.

Favor Giver. As I began playing sports, I was concerned that God be on my side, passing out favors in the form of victories. Only much later did it occur to me to wonder if I were on God's side. Now I know God always is on my side and everyone else's because being on my side does not exclude him from being on the side of another. Life is not made up of winners and losers from God's perspective.

I prayed for hits in baseball and for making free throws in basketball.

Interestingly, I did not pray to avoid errors or pray to make field goals in basketball. The action was too intense to think about praying at those times. I prayed for my team to win and arrogantly assumed God would reward me because I prayed, read the Bible, and went to church. God was indebted to me; he owed me some favors. I was sure no one on the other teams could match such a performance. Maybe not, but their athletic performance often was better than mine, and I discovered that was what made the difference in winning and losing sports events. I concluded that who won ball games was not God's concern.

Gap Filler. About the time I went to college, my view of God changed somewhat from that of being a favor giver to being a rather distant creature, aloof and removed from life. He knew all that was going on as well as everything I thought, said, and did. Since he already knew all, I saw no reason to spend my energy communicating my needs to him. Jesus had said that God knew my needs even before I did, so why bother? Although God was distant, I would never have said that he was absent. I thought he was still at my beck and call to come in and snatch me out of threatening situations. He also was convenient for filling in the gaps in my comprehension of life. Whatever I could not explain, I just filled in by saying, "God did it." This is really a five-year-old mentality. Ask a four- or five-year-old, "Who made the car?" Often the response is, "God did."

My thinking processes expanded in many areas, but when it came to understanding what God was like, I kept him as small as possible, perhaps as a way to control him. Had I let God be too big I might not have known what to do with him. Besides, there was a secure feeling in knowing how God functioned and where he fit into the scheme of things.

Contender. Then I enrolled in a college Old Testament survey course. I can still feel the agony of those first six weeks of class. I can see myself walking around the campus in a daze. The professor, B. A. Sizemore, very gently was encouraging me to take the Bible seriously. Flexibility may have characterized my approach toward learning in other areas, but when it came to the Bible and God, rigidity was my security, although I would not admit it.

Some of my most meaningful praying occurred during those six weeks, although I did not call it praying at the time. I was in agony, conflict, struggle too deep for words, but the Spirit was pleading my case with God. Everything seemed to be up for review and reconsideration in my life: my vocational choice, my marital choice, my view of God, my view of the world, and my view of myself. I had put God in a box and was planning on keeping him there for the rest of my life. I had determined how God would function. I was wrestling with the God in whom I had believed. Out of the fuzziness of all of this struggle came a glimmer of light in the form of a question, If God were what I claimed him to be, namely God, and if he could do all I said I believed he could do, namely create this universe and other universes, then why was I setting limits on how and when he did all of this? I had been like a turtle tightly shut up in my shell, but, ever so slightly, I began to stick out my head and neck. I was becoming teachable in my understanding of and communion with God. In struggling with my view of God, I was struggling with my concept of prayer and vice versa. God had been my Contender.

Friend. I began asking, What is God like? The answer seemed to be in Christ. As I searched the Gospels, I saw a loving Father, a compassionate Friend, rather than the contender of earlier days. Suddenly the Exodus statement about God speaking to Moses as a friend (33:11) leaped off the page. Certainly God is beyond us, greater than and more than we ever can comprehend. Yet, he also is present with us and to us as a friend of the highest order. Jesus portrayed God as a loving Father and intimate Friend. The more my view of God is one of a loving Father, the better able I am to commune with him. The more like Santa Claus, Angry Old Man, Favor Giver, Gap Filler, or Contender I perceive him to be, the more distance I want from him and the less able I am to communicate with him. With an intimate friend I will share anything and everything. God as shown in Christ is an intimate friend par excellence.

A significant development in my personal growth has occurred as a result of my struggle with prayer. As my view of God has moved toward knowing him as a loving Father and intimate Friend, the meaning and value of prayer has increased, and my view of myself has improved.

There is a direct correlation between what God is like, the significance of prayer, and self-esteem.

Note

1. Elton Trueblood, *The Lord's Prayers* (New York: Harper & Row, 1965), p. 26.

3

Learning to Pray
for Friends and Enemies

Greater love has no man than this, that a man lay down his life for his friends. You are my friends if you do what I command you. No longer do I call you servants, for the servant does not know what his master is doing; but I have called you friends, for all that I have heard from my Father I have made known to you (John 15:13-15).

But I say to you, love your enemies and pray for those who persecute you, so that you may be sons of your Father who is in heaven; for he makes his sun rise on the evil and on the good, and sends rain on the just and on the unjust (Matt. 5:44-45).

Petitionary Prayer

Prayer is basically petition—making requests, seeking guidance, asking for the attention of God. Prayer also is praise, thanksgiving, and confession, but petition is at the heart of prayer.[1]

Long before the *Reader's Digest* published a condensed Bible, I had been reading my own condensed version of Scripture. I condensed the "begat" sections because they never did inspire me. Other sections I omitted because I was too uncomfortable with them. Jeremiah's approach to God is hardly the way I learned to talk to God:

> Cursed be the day
>   on which I was born!
> The day when my mother bore me,
>   let it not be blessed!
> Cursed be the man
>   who brought the news to my father,
> "A son is born to you,"
>   making him very glad (Jer. 20:14-15).

If I ever thought of shaking my fist at God, I quickly repressed such a thought, but not Jeremiah.

> Why is my pain unceasing,
>   my wound incurable,
>   refusing to be healed?
> Wilt thou be to me like a deceitful brook,
>   like waters that fail? (Jer. 15:18).

Even with the Psalms, a condensed version is preferred by many. Who would dare pray,

> Rouse thyself! Why sleepest thou, O Lord?
>   Awake! Do not cast us off for ever!
> Why dost thou hide thy face?
>   Why dost thou forget our affliction and oppression? (Ps. 44:23-24).

Prayers such as these indicate a familiarity and a presumptuousness that make us uncomfortable. The chief presumption is that we can commune at all with God. Once we are over that hurdle, we are at least on our way to courageous and confrontive dialogue with God.

Rather than understanding prayer as communion with God, we have viewed prayer, and especially petitionary prayer, as an attempt to bend the will of God. This approach has been built on the assumption that human will and God's will always are in conflict. When prayer is based on this assumption, the only way out is to speak the magic phrase, "Not my will but thine be done." Then whatever happens is interpreted as God's will. Many people have died of disease and family members have concluded, "It was God's will." What about the medical team that worked so hard on the side of health and wholeness? Were they working against God's will? If they were, then why is God so cruel as to have people expend the best they have for nothing?

We need to consider petitionary prayer from the position of communication rather than will. A key to understanding prayer as communication is Jesus' prayer in the garden of Gethsemane. This is really the Lord's prayer with regard to his personal anguish and need. Mark describes Jesus as being "greatly distressed and troubled." He had his disciples to "sit here" and then took Peter, James, and John further into the garden and instructed them to "remain here, and watch," indicating that they were to guard the place and protect him from intrusion while he prayed (14:32-42). This conveys both the mounting threat that Jesus sensed and his need to commune with the Father.

Jesus prayed, "Abba, Father, all things are possible to thee; remove this cup from me; yet not what I will, but what thou wilt." Jesus' use of "Abba" is the address of intimacy of a child to his father. It expresses the closeness, warmth, and understanding that exists in a relationship where each knows and is known by the other. "All things are possible to thee." What were some of the possibilities at this point? Jesus could have escaped into the darkness. The religious leaders could have been converted. Perhaps there could have been more time. Judas could have changed his mind. Pilate could have had the courage to take a stand. The crowd could have asked for Jesus to have been released. These were some of the possibilities.

The second part of this prayer is, "Remove this cup from me." Jesus was astute to the emotional and political climate. His reading of life told him that his conflict with the religious leaders was reaching a climax, and it was apparent to him that his life would be on the block. He did not want to die, and he said so when he demanded, "Remove this cup from me." The verb, "remove," is in the imperative mood. Our tendency is to quote this line of the prayer in a soft, sweet whisper, but spoken in the imperative mood it expresses the great agony of one who does not want to die but sees his death about to become a reality.

This was the prayer of one who felt he had little or no control of the situation. He was saying that it is acceptable to be afraid and it is acceptable to want to avoid suffering, pain, and misery. Although we admit that Jesus was human, do we not have difficulty permitting him to be human enough to be afraid, to dread suffering, or to desire for the course he is traveling to be altered? Here is an example of courageous, presumptuous, demanding prayer, "Remove this cup from me," perhaps spoken with a shout of emotion. It illustrates the open communication of intimacy between Jesus and God, the kind of intimacy Jesus encouraged his disciples to develop. If their praying were to have any value and integrity, they needed this kind of intimacy with God.

The phrase, "Yet not what I will, but what thou wilt," spoken forcefully by Jesus, has become an expression of sad resignation when spoken by those who then identify whatever happens as God's will. In this way, people have blamed God for many unjust acts, including murder, extortion, and prejudice. Mark makes the point that this phrase was neither sad resignation nor submission for Jesus by recording the fact that Jesus prayed the same prayer three times. After considering all the possibilities and making his appeal that his life not end then, Jesus could say, "Not what I will, but what thou wilt." Jesus was free to express his urgent desires to his Father, and his Father was free to respond. Then, Jesus was free to accept or reject the Father's response. This utterance, "What thou wilt," was voluntary, rather than the result of a trap that God had set in which Jesus was caught.

Jesus' prayer indicated his need to say what he wanted and the importance of saying no to some things before feeling freed to say yes. I am reminded of an experience that occurred while I was weighing the factors involved in leaving one pastorate to accept another. Through intensive discussions with the search committee and an open meeting with the congregation, many issues were raised and emotions exposed, both for the congregation and for me. As the concerns began to bombard me, I wrestled with the options. The day before a recommendation was to go from the search committee to the congregation, I came to a decision and called the chairperson to request that my name be withdrawn from consideration. I had anticipated the variety of ways she might respond to my request. However, I had not contemplated her response, "Don't you want to think about that a little more?" How ridiculous! For days I had not been able to think about anything else; yet, her question was surprising.

I was so sure I could call her back in a few hours to tell her my decision was firm that I said, "OK. I'll think about it a little more." Barely had I put down the receiver before the fog began to clear from my mind. It seemed only fair to them and to me that we see each other again in the process of making a decision. Before long I called the chairperson again to tell her to proceed with the recommendation. The possibility of my becoming their pastor was then contigent upon another visit with the congregation and their vote concerning me. In this instance, I had to say no before I could say yes; saying no served as a catalyst for even more intense struggle and a stronger ability to say yes. I then felt free to decide either way concerning a job change. Similarly, some spouses describe a time in their dating and courtship when they said no to the ones they eventually married. Saying no freed them enough from the situation to enable them to be more objective about their relationships and about the meaning and value of marriage for them.

What is basic in petitionary prayer is the concept and comprehension that the pray-er is communicating with God, regardless of the name used to identify God. Through this communication process, the doors of the possible begin to open. Many of the psalms begin in despair, but within them there is a turning point as the psalmist began to be open to the possible. Notice the despair in the first part of Psalm 13:

> How long, O Lord? Wilt thou forget me for ever?
> How long wilt thou hide thy face from me?
> How long must I bear pain in my soul,
>   and have sorrow in my heart all the day?
> How long shall my enemy be exalted over me?
> Consider and answer me, O Lord my God;
>   lighten my eyes, lest I sleep the sleep of death;
> lest my enemy say, "I have prevailed over him";
>   lest my foes rejoice because I am shaken (vv. 1-4).

Here is the transition for the psalmist:

> But I have trusted in thy steadfast love;
>   my heart shall rejoice in thy salvation.
> I will sing to the Lord,
>   because he has dealt bountifully with me (vv. 5-6).

I suspect that every person who has ever prayed has been disappointed when what was prayed for didn't occur. Some wave another magic phrase, "It wasn't God's will," as the catchall explanation.

A significant question is, Why do people pray? The primary reason is because they are convinced that God listens to them.[2] The converse is also true. People stop praying because they are convinced that God doesn't listen to them anymore. People need assurance of an audience with God in order to continue communing with him. A study done by David Elkind suggests that the opportunity to communicate with God about one's needs and struggles may be more important than evidence that a person's prayers have been answered.[3]

The earlier examples from Jeremiah and the psalms suggest that in prayer, specifically in petitionary prayer, we need to focus on the communication process and address the transaction rather than the motivations behind the transaction.[4] Theodore Newcomb's ideas on coorientation[5] are helpful with regard to the significance of prayer being communication rather than a conflict of wills in which we are embattled with God. Coorientation is the ability to orient oneself to the subject of discussion and to another's anticipated view of this subject simultaneously. Coorientation is not seeing eye to eye. Rather, it is the ability to view a situation from the perspective of another.

For example, I know how Peggy, my wife, will respond on an issue affecting our relationship to each other. I may imagine what I will say, anticipate what her response will be, and then contemplate my response to her response. Coorientation may involve verbal exchange, but that is not necessary. Coorientation occurred as I anticipated the conversation with the chairperson of the pastor search committee mentioned earlier. In human relationships, real difficulties arise when we fail to check out our coorientation perceptions by verbalizing them and determining whether our comprehension of the other is correct or prejudiced.

With regard to prayer, we are able to express our needs, desires, and problems to God and, at the same time, anticipate how God will respond. Our anticipation will be influenced by our view of God and our self-esteem. Our anticipation ought also to be informed by how God responded to others, including Jesus and the biblical persons, as well as the church fathers and well-known devotionalists, including Francis of Assisi, John Woolman, Thomas Kelly, and Michael Quoist.

Another way for our anticipation to be informed is to ask ourselves whether the response expected from God portrays him more like a loving friend or an angry beast. The closer the anticipated response is to a loving friend, the more nearly correct we are in our coorientation. When communicating with God in this manner, we may urge God to respond in a specific way and at the same time doubt that God will respond in the way we have requested. The following prayer illustrates this point:

God,

Those people give me fits. Nothing I do meets their approval. Always they are looking, hoping I'll make a mistake. They sit like vultures waiting to pounce on my carcass when I stumble.

Why don't you change their attitudes? Why don't you give them loving attitudes of warmth and acceptance? If you can't or won't do that, why don't you urge them to go elsewhere instead of harassing me?

Have you ever prayed such a prayer? Have you ever had such thoughts? In a sense, you have prayed this kind of prayer if you have had thoughts like these. Our minds are working all the time, whether we are awake or asleep. We think thoughts we cannot control, and they interfere with the best intentions. Thinking is unceasing. We struggle with how to convert our unceasing thinking into unceasing praying. Unceasing prayer neither means thinking about God every moment nor babbling to him constantly. To pray unceasingly is to realize that all of our thoughts occur in the presence of God. We need to turn all our thoughts into conversations with God, conversations that may or may not be verbal. Then the significant question is not, What do I think? but rather, To whom do I offer my thoughts?

This seems to be the understanding of people in the Old Testament. They talked to God as if their suffering did not matter to him. When relief from their suffering was delayed, they accused God of a lack of compassion. When their enemies were suffering, they rejoiced, saying that God was punishing them for mistreating the Israelites. They tried to bargain with God, using different approaches to get the responses they wanted. They played up to his name, his reputation, his promises. Anything goes in an effort to convince God that he must do something to help in an otherwise hopeless situation.

Evident in the prayers of people in the Old Testament is the free-flow-for-all. Unlike them, we fail or refuse to let our prayers flow directly from ourselves without censoring them. We think we have to get the theology straight in order to commune with God, exchanging one magic formula for another.

There is evidence of this free flow in the prayers of Jesus and his courageous approach to God, as he spoke imperatively and freely, letting his fears and feelings be known. There is potential peril in the free flow of prayer that releases emotions within us of which we often are unaware. As we explore ourselves through prayer, we need to realize that it is God who is calling to consciousness the infinite possibilities within us. We are not seeking God; rather, God seeks us and our search is a response to the Creator who has been brooding and moving over us since the day of our creation.

This free flow of thoughts presented to God changes the whole stance of prayer from the position where the pray-er is in opposition to God's will and must finally submit to him in static monologue to the position of communicating freely in dynamic dialogue with God. Then one is free to accept or reject the Father's response. Such freedom is frightening. We prefer to submit to a will that conflicts with ours because that enables us to resign from any responsibility for what happens in our lives.

This became most clear to me in 1977 when I was being considered for the position of pastor of Broadview Baptist Church. In discussions prior to a vote being taken, some issues had been raised that were painful and difficult. I knew there would be some negative votes, and it became important to me to settle on how many negative votes would cause me to say no if I received the invitation to be pastor. After much thought and evaluation, I concluded that fifty negative votes was the critical number. More than fifty negative votes would cause me seriously to consider saying no. Less than fifty negative votes would cause me seriously to consider saying yes. When the invitation came, fifty negative votes had been cast. That was frightening to me because then I was free to remain at my present church or move to another. The decision was mine. Where did I want to work? God would be with me at either place.

Praying for Friends

Against the backdrop of petitionary prayer, I now focus on learning to pray for friends. Initially, you may think that friends are the easiest people for whom to pray and that such prayers are easily formed and expressed. That is what I thought, too, as I seriously began thinking about and desiring to pray for my friends. After all, my friends' concerns readily become my own, don't they?

Friendship may begin with distance and aloofness. Often there is a period of emotional sparring where each checks out the other by keeping his "hand close to his chest." As trust and acceptance develop, more risks are taken; the two share more of themselves in usually pleasant, joyful experiences at first. Bonding occurs as they discover common backgrounds or interests. Then they are able to risk sharing some struggles, even some deep wounds, and eventually some failures. In this process, some things are glossed over; namely, the negative attributes of friends. Why? Because we are afraid those negative attributes will become barriers to the friendship and perhaps also they are similar to negative attributes in ourselves that we are hesitant to admit. Identifying with friends reveals positive and negative qualities in the friends and in ourselves.

Types of Friends

Friends come in a variety of types. No doubt each person has his own way of identifying the kinds of friends he has. I am listing five types of friends. One friend probably has all of the characteristics mentioned in these five types, although in each friend one characteristic seems more dominant than the others.

Colleague. The use of the word basically means a fellow worker in the same profession. Technically, all ministers are my colleagues.

I am using *colleague* in an even more limited sense to mean a fellow minister with whom I have developed a high trust level and who mutually shares with me the joys and struggles of being a minister. Because he is in the same profession, he knows what work can be like for me and has insight and understanding. He can laugh with me when I laugh and cry with me when I cry.

Learning to pray for a colleague involves being able to identify feelings and needs I have had in a similar situation or projecting what my feelings and needs might be were my circumstances like his. One colleague, Ralph, is a thirty-six-year-old minister. His many pastoral skills include sensitivity to individual needs and the ability to see the community as his parish. As a result of mounting frustration, increasing conflicts, and dead-end solutions, Ralph resigned as pastor of a church and was uncertain of employment. Out of my concern for him I offered this prayer:

The pastorate lost a good man on Easter, Lord.

It's strange that crucifixion happened in the church and on Easter. I guess we still believe more in crucifixion than we do in resurrection. At least that is the method we choose to deal with persons whose leadership we dislike.

Not everybody could do what Ralph does, Father. He not only survives in a small town but he actually ministers to people there.

He is a pastor to many who are outside the church. He really sees the community as his parish. He is involved in the Kiwanis Club and Little League baseball, ministering to people in those organizations, as well as to those in the church. There is a sense in which he is appreciated and respected more by the community than by the church. It's an old scenario repeated more often than I like to admit.

God, Ralph couldn't take it any longer. He had to get out of the pastorate. He felt no support from the congregation. How devastating! He quit with no place to work but with five bodies to feed, clothe, and shelter. Was he crazy or courageous? I think he was courageous. I couldn't have done it.

Ralph will always be a pastor, won't he, Father? That's what he knows how to do, and he likes ministering to people. He's had it with the church, and I don't blame him. He is angry. I would be, too. Father, don't let his anger sour and turn to bitterness. He resents that congregation. Help Ralph, Father, to deal appropriately with his resentment so that all of his life is not jaundiced by it.

Father, you have come to many people through Ralph. There are many others to whom you can come through him. May Ralph continue to desire to be your messenger to others. Amen.

Ralph has since become a pastoral counselor in a counseling center. He is being a pastor, a messenger of God to others—just not in the traditional congregational setting. He is a colleague for whom I am learning to pray.

Confidant. One of the most vital services a friend provides is that of being a confidant. Within the word is its root word, *confide,* which means "to trust with." A confidant is one with whom I trust my deepest and darkest secrets and fears. It is self-destructive to carry around inside myself my darkest secrets and fears. One of the best ways to explode fantasies is to put them into words. One of the best ways for fantasies to become destructive is to keep them to oneself, feeding them and feeding on them. One of my premises for the value of prayer is that everybody needs an audience. Everyone needs someone who will listen with interest to what one needs and feels. Prayer is directed to God because he has created us and promised to listen to us. The belief that God hears me in my agony and ecstasy is concretized in a confidant. In this kind of friendship, God is incarnate as we become priests to each other. Was this not part of what Jesus had in mind when he invited people to be his disciples? Mark records, "And he went up on the mountain, and called to him those whom he desired; and they came to him. And he appointed twelve, to be with him, and to be sent out to preach and have authority to cast out demons" (Mark 3:13-15). According to Mark, one reason Jesus chose the twelve was the value of their friendship to him. Were not the twelve that inner circle of friends with whom Jesus shared his most intimate struggles? Did not Peter, James, and John become Jesus' confidants as the ministry unfolded, the pressures mounted, and the enemies increased?

My initial reaction to a confidant is that of indebtedness because he has listened to me. That may create distance, lead to a shallow relationship, and result in superficial praying. When I get beyond the indebted feeling in praying for a confidant, I begin to pray for the confidant and learn about myself simultaneously. One of my confidants is my wife, Peggy. The following prayer illustrates the simultaneousness of praying and learning.

Father,
Because of the depth of my love for Peggy, I want to give her

the very best. Hallmark just can't put my feelings into words. I have found that dialogue with you often digs deep into the wellspring of my being and brings up latent feelings of vitality, frustration, and gratitude. I want to talk to you, Lord, about Peggy.

Suddenly I need to talk to you about me before I can talk about her. I'm so hard to live with. I'm so logical, always thinking before acting, controlled, pushed, or driven. I schedule, organize, straighten. What compulsion! Who could put up with all of this? Sometimes I can't stand myself. But Peggy puts up with me, not without aggravation and frustration, but she puts up with me, and I'm glad she does.

Lord, you know that Peggy is hard to live with. She is so spontaneous, often acting without thinking, usually willing to say yes, seldom able to say no, stretching herself to the breaking point but not breaking, yet. She tries so hard to receive my approval. Have I put that on her with my scowls and sighs, my ranting and raving? Please forgive me, Lord. Help Peggy to forgive me too.

Sixteen years we've known each other. It was her eyes that first caught my attention. Their bright blueness conveyed aliveness. They were windows into her life. They still are! Her eyes also are mirrors often reflecting her feelings about me—unsure, delighted, insecure, warm, angry, joyful, sensual. Help her to keep speaking to me with her eyes and her words. Help me to hear her with my ears and my heart.

Life has gotten better and better and harder and harder for us. Our third month of marriage was the pits. Suddenly we didn't know who we had married. I thought it was all over. I thought, *If marriage is going to be like this, it ought to be over.* With your help, Father, we made it back from the abyss of shattered dreams.

Our lives were simpler those first years. Getting time alone together was easy. Debriefing each other about the day in class or at work was fun. Then it was just the two of us. Now we have added Melanie, Danita, and Brandon, and a dog, a bird, and a rabbit. There have been gerbils and hamsters. No doubt there will be again, and who knows what else? Life is harder now, but it also is better. We enjoy the kids most of the time. Looking at life from their level is intriguing. They enjoy us most of the time. They certainly call for us to be honest with them and with each other. Sometimes that is painful but always helpful. Thank you, Father, for teaching us through our children.

Peggy has filled her life with wifing, mothering, teaching, singing, acting, and churching. She expresses purpose and meaning in life through these channels. Vacuuming, washing, and dusting just don't give her much satisfaction. I can understand that. I don't find any fulfillment in these mundane, routine things.

It bothers me not, Lord, that Peggy will climb some mountain that I haven't climbed because she will describe the view for me. O Father, often we get our lives filled with activities and only pass in the night. Then we scream at each other, usually because we are screaming for each other. Help us to see that.

No one knows me better than Peggy. No one has had more influence on my life than she. No one challenges and confronts me like she does. No one comforts and supports me like she does. No one can cut through my defenses like she can. No one admires and respects me more than she does. No one gets more frustrated with me than she does. No one loves me more than she does. And there is no one I love more than I love her.

For thirteen years we have been in the pits and on the peaks together. The future promises more pits and more peaks. There is no one I would rather be in the pits and on the peaks with than Peggy. Thank you, God, for her. Thank you, God, for me. And thank you for us. Amen.

Learning to pray for a confidant becomes an intimate interaction with God about one who is making a large contribution to the person the pray-er is. I often am not conscious of the influence and contribution another is making to my life until I begin turning my thoughts about that person into conversation with God. I also discover that what is happening in a confidant's life becomes a concern of my own and events of the day are interrupted with thoughts about him. Taking time to center my concerns for him and communicate them to God eases my anxiety and causes me to be more cognizant of how and why he is so important to me. Thus, his needs become like my own. Here is an example:

Father,

What a friend I have in Joe. He is willing to hear my frustrations, aggravations, and my excitement and joy. In his style, he has taught me to be more candid. He is a maverick according to traditional clergy role and expectations. Sometimes people so label him as a way to avoid dealing with his challenges. Rejection is hard to take, however it comes. Thank you for keeping Joe from being resentful or bitter.

Joe taught me to leave written prayers with people as a ministry. I have found this a valuable tool. Thank you for teaching me through Joe.

Today, Lord, I am most concerned about Joe because he is preparing for surgery. No matter how routine surgery is, when it is happening to someone as important to me as Joe, I am concerned, a little frightened, for him. I want the surgery to be successful, and I want the time of recuperation to be rapid and profitable for Joe.

Lord, I have read that you were a friend to Abraham. Paul said that even when life caved in on him he was not without a friend. I feel that way about Joe. His friendship is a parable to me about the friendship above time. Thank you, Father, for the gift of Joe's friendship and for what it tells me about your friendship to all of us. Amen.

Confronter. The most disturbing kind of friend for me to have is one who confronts me with his perception of me. I react to confrontation with fear or anger. Because a friend perceives me as imperfect, needing work in some area of my life, or having been completely wrong in a deed or decision, I fear he will have nothing to do with me unless I change my ways. Thomas Merton said a person seeks only one thing more than happiness, and that is approval. When a friend becomes confrontive, I am fearful of losing a friend. What relief comes as I discover that confrontation and rejection are not the same!

My other response to confrontation is anger. I feel attacked and I become defensive. What kind of friend is this who challenges what I say or do? I need and want support, not challenge. Emotionally, I often equate support with agreement, especially in a situation or with an issue with which I am struggling. For a friend to be confrontive causes me unjustifiably to question his friendship.

My ability to pray for my confronter helps me to process my feelings, to evaluate his perceptions, and to deepen the friendship.

God, anyone could draw a graph of my joys and pains by looking at a record of my telephone calls to John. He is the friend of my extremes. I call him when I'm flying high or crawling low. Why do I think of him at those times? He seems to be part of life's balancing act for me. I'm never quite as high or quite as low at the end of our conversations as I was at the beginning. John seems to be able to mirror reality for me. Usually that is what I need. I'm glad he cares enough to risk my rejecting him in order to confront me, which is what I need, rather than to give me back-slapping pablum, which is what I want.

What surprises me, Father, about John is that time lag is never a problem. Regardless of the time and events that have transpired between calls, as soon as there is telephone contact, there is emotional connection. We get on the same frequency immediately. What John offers is seldom what I want but is invariably what I need. Maybe that is why I think of him at high and low tides. Thank you, Father, for the confrontive friend that John is. Amen.

Mentor. In Homer's *Odyssey,* Odysseus's loyal friend and wise adviser was Mentor. When Odysseus left home for the Trojan War, he asked Mentor to look after his son, Telemachus. Telemachus had a formal arrangement with his adviser. Many today have similar arrangements with their mentors, but this has not been the case for me. I am discovering my mentors in retrospect. Rather than having a single mentor, I have had several. My grandfather gave me my earliest view of healthy religion. Neither he nor I knew he was doing this for me. Three seminary professors have been my mentors during different stages of my development.

One of the common threads in my four pastorates is that I have had a mentor in each place. Only now as I write this am I conscious of these church mentors. In each congregation, I have developed a relationship with someone who has been a member of the congregation for many years. Each of these persons provided me with wise counsel in understanding the congregation, its history and traditions, as well as helpful suggestions about how to resolve conflict in the congregation. Having a mentor is a two-way relationship. Through mutual sharing I have become aware of some of the needs of my mentors. The following prayer reveals some things about one of them, some of my concerns for him, and indicates how some things I see in him raise issues about myself:

Apparently George has always been a private person, Lord. I'm concerned about him, Lord. Is he getting what's coming to him? That seems to be my question, not his. I am amazed at his coping ability in the face of financial difficulty. He has drawn a great deal of strength from his family. He says he had his day in the sun and enjoyed it. Now life is moving in another direction. Is it better to have had and lost than never to have had at all? George seems to think so. I don't know that I could have the same outlook if I were in his situation.

God, I do like George a lot. He knows what church is and who church is. You speak to me every time I see him. I wish he were attending worship, but I guess that's just too public for him now. It may be too public for him forever. He is a member of my private church. Thank you, Father, for George. Amen.

Model. Each of us probably is modeling something for another. One of the reasons I develop a friendship is because of characteristics I see in another which I like. As the friendship grows, I begin emulating one or more of those characteristics by "trying them on for size" to see how they fit me.

We probably are eclectic in our modeling, trying on characteristics from diverse friends. One of the traps of modeling is the temptation to become a clone, destroying one's authenticity and integrity.

It has been by encountering friends who would talk openly about their feelings, their relationships with others, their disappointments, dreams, and plans that I am learning to be able to do the same. Both consciously and unconsciously, I see things in their lives and apply them in mine. I suspect that the modeling goes the other way also. I think it is helpful, healthy, and bonding for a person to tell another when and what he has learned from him. My attitude is one of gratitude for friends who have been models for me.

Father,

I am richly blessed with friends. I really don't know what life would be like without friends. Each contributes to who I am.

Joan has the uncanny ability to speak a word of encouragement at just the right time. There are many days when I am certain that were it not for her I would not be able to survive here. Thank you for communicating encouragement to me through Joan.

Steve has contributed to my growth through his confessional preaching. Thank you for giving him that gift and for enabling him to make himself vulnerable for the benefit of others.

Ruth seems to bring out the playful child in me. In her presence I enjoy turning loose my cynical, sarcastic self. Ruth seems to have no role expectations of me. She allows, wants, insists that I be myself with her. That is refreshing, relaxing, and renewing. Thank you for Ruth's no-strings-attached friendship.

Father, I am grateful for Monica's availability. Our mutual sharing is healthy and helpful and has incarnated the truth of burden bearing. Her openness and honesty are so refreshing. There is no pretense with her. I need more friends like her. I need to be more like her.

For these named friends and for the multitude of unnamed friends, I am deeply grateful. I have just begun to realize how important these relationships are to my emotional well-being and to my understanding and relationship to you, Father. Thank you for wrapping and sending your availability in Joan, Steve, Ruth, and Monica. I trust that you will wrap and send one of your gifts through me to others. Amen.

Probably everybody knows someone who seems to epitomize friend-ship for them. This person seems to convey friendship in every relationship and to demonstrate qualities that any friend would like to have. The following prayer expresses gratitude for one who does this for me.

Father,

I am sure that when you look at Carl Greisser you are pleased with who you see. You have done a very good work in him. Thank you, Father, for Carl.

Carl's humor, generosity, and sense of adventure are special gifts you have given him, Father. His sense of humor is contagious. Carl always has a joke to tell. He shows warmth and affection by teasing, chiding, and joking with those who are important to him. Thank you for his sense of humor.

Carl has a generous spirit. He is willing to share what he has, rather than keep it for himself. Most of all, he is willing to share his laughter and his love. When these gifts are shared, others want to share in kind. We need more people like Carl, Father. Thank you for his generosity.

I like Carl's enthusiasm for adventure—hitchhiking across the country as a college student, roller skating at sixty-five, sled riding at seventy, diving from the high board at seventy-six. He is a man very much alive and enjoying it. I like that. Thank you for his adventurous spirit.

Lord, I am grateful for the quality and quantity of Carl's life now spanning nearly fourscore years. He's done a lot of living in seventy-eight years. He's known poverty that necessitated spreading jelly thin and looking for a lost penny until it was found. He's had joy—getting a college scholarship was one. He's had sadness—hurting his arm and having to quit pitching a baseball. God, that must have been hard for him. Maybe he never quite got over it. Comfort him from this and other hurts. Thank you for the living Carl has done and for the living he has yet to do.

Father, you really have done a good work in Carl Greisser. Thank you for who he has been to so many. Thank you for who he is to me. Amen.

Learning to pray for friends has increased the value of friendship for me and has helped me discover friends I did not know I had or was taking for granted. Awareness of friends also has caused me to examine the kind of friend I am, the kind of friend I want to be, and to discover at least partially what is involved in getting from where I am to where I want to be.

Praying for Enemies

Having enemies is not easy to admit. A part of me believes that if I have enemies it is because I have done something wrong. Most of the enemies I have are in the church, probably because that is where I invest most of my time and energy. Learning that I had enemies in the church shattered the idealism that I could work and relate well to anyone. I should have known better. Even Jesus couldn't do that.

Just as friendship requires contributions from two people, it also takes two to have differences that become enmity between them. I have contributed to my enemies being my enemies. To be able to pray for my enemies is a major growth step because it is an admission of having enemies and knowing who they are.

Jesus questioned, "For if you love those who love you, what reward have you? Do not even the tax collectors do the same? And if you salute only your brethren, what more are you doing than others? Do not even the Gentiles do the same?" (Matt. 5:46-47). Isn't Jesus suggesting that for me to pray for my enemies will affect how I relate to them?

To pray for enemies calls to my awareness some frightening personal feelings. Communicating these feelings to God helps me empathize with my enemies. There is a sense in which my enemies represent my shadow side. To begin to know my enemies is to learn some things about my darker side. Because my enemies represent something of my shadow side, I need to keep in mind that I probably represent some of their shadow sides. The animosity an enemy has for me probably is not all because of me but includes both who or what I represent and of whom I remind him.

Types of Enemies

I have identified five types of enemies: skeptic, competitor, detractor, betrayer, and antagonist. My list of enemy types is by no means exhaustive. I am certain you can add to this list or find words that are more descriptive for you. I hope you will because the more specific you and I can be in identifying our enemies and what they are like, the better will be our learning to pray for them.

Skeptic. When I suggest that a skeptic is an enemy, I am using the term to identify the person who has become disenchanted with me because of an issue, or just basically doesn't like me, and then continually finds fault with me. Several years ago a worship survey was done in a church where I was pastor. One person registered the complaint that he didn't like for me to read the prayers I offered during worship service. I had not written a prayer for worship for at least six months prior to the survey. Perhaps this person did not like the structure and order of the worship service and was identifying an area that he thought would get the worship committee's attention.

The skeptic mistrusts me and functions as a sniper. He takes shots at me before other people but does not say anything to me. I think public figures are most likely to have this kind of enemy. This enemy type may be more prevalent in the church than anywhere. Although this enemy says nothing to me directly, silence may be a cue. Eventually the message will begin to get to me. Here is a prayer I offered for one skeptic.

Father,

I really don't know what to do about Marian or with her. I am convinced that nothing I do is satisfactory to her. It seems so difficult for her when she realizes how differently she and I see an issue or understand a passage of Scripture. I guess she equates acceptance with agreement. I used to do that too.

I think freedom is difficult for Marian, too, Father. If all of life could just be orderly and structured so there would be no surprises, she would be more at ease. But life isn't that way. Is there any way I can help her with this struggle? Will Marian trust me enough to permit us to struggle together? I wish she would, but I doubt if it will ever happen. Thanks for listening. Amen.

Competitor. Culture has encouraged, often demanded, that we live in the comparative mood. The comparative mood leads to the competitive mood, as we discover that we do not measure up to whomever we compare ourselves. Then, when jealousy and envy set in, we move into the destructive mood. The jealous competitor says, "If I don't have what you have, I will fight you every step of the way to make you miserable." The envious competitor says, "If I can't have what you have, I'll destroy you so you can't have it either." The only comparison that should be done is comparing one's performance to one's potential. This was Paul's suggestion to the Galatians. "But let each one test his own work, and then his reason to boast will be in himself alone and not in his neighbor" (6:4).

The competitor may actively seek support from others for his position and use that support as evidence that my position is wrong. Or he may be more subtle in his approach, managing to get others to work behind the scenes while he appears "holy" and "righteous" to all who hear and see him:

Father,

I don't like Sam's scowl. He seems so unhappy, so angry. At times I am convinced he hates me. There are times when I am certain he would delight in destroying me. Please protect me from allowing my paranoia to rule me.

I have trouble admitting there is someone to whom I can't minister, but Sam is one. I do not struggle much when someone disagrees with me, but sugar-coated, mean-spirited disagreement is hard for me to handle. I get angry. I feel threatened. I do a lot of looking over my shoulder. There was a time when I was immobilized, but you helped me through that. I thought things would get better, and they have. I guess I wanted things to get well, and that may never happen. I feel better admitting that. It really hurts when Sam avoids speaking to me. Is there a part of me that is like him? If so, help me to change. Deliver me from doing to Sam what I feel he has done to me. Amen.

Detractor. Regardless of what my task or objective, there usually is someone attempting to divert my attention from that objective. On one occasion in Jesus' ministry, Peter was the detractor. Jesus said to him, "Get behind me, Satan! You are a hindrance to me; for you are not on the side of God, but of men" (Matt. 16:23). The detractor may be one who is so emotionally needy that he is calling selfishly for time and attention for himself that diverts energy away from others. Jealousy may be part of the dynamic involved. Or a detractor may be more forthright and conscious of his actions. He has set an agenda for me and continually is attempting to get me to pursue his set of priorities which are more in line with what he thinks I should be doing.

In the church, the detractor often wraps his cause in the pious language of missions or evangelism in the narrowest definition of these concepts. A detractor can divert all of the energy and attention of the congregation away from its objective. For me, the most difficult thing to do in dealing with a detractor is to be angry but not sin. The primary tool of a detractor is manipulation, and I get angry when I am being manipulated. Being able to name these things in communion with God helps me deal with a detractor.

Father,

I know that Earl is dissatisfied with me. Some days I feel that the only solution is to call him up and ask what he thinks I should do today. Whatever I do without his consent I know will be wrong. Why is he like this? Why does everything always have to go Earl's way or be judged worthless, if not verbally, then by his actions and facial expressions? I get so angry with him, I just want to lash out at him. Sometimes I'm afraid I'll lose control of myself and verbally unload on him in public. My private conversations with Earl have gotten me nowhere.

Treating him with kindness has helped me. Of course, sometimes my kindness has been a sarcastic, I'll-fix-you attitude. Forgive me for that, Father. Help me to communicate genuine concern for him. Make him aware of some of the pain he causes me and others with his diversions and detractions. Amen.

Betrayer. It may be that the most painful hurt a person ever experiences is that of betrayal. To trust another, whether with confidential information or with a life commitment, and have that trust broken is painful and emotionally debilitating. A betrayal experience tends to declare all of one's life null and void. When someone who was trusted has broken that trust, a friend can become an enemy. The following prayer expresses the gamut of feelings that mushroom from encounter with a betrayer. It often is difficult to get to the point in prayer. Notice in this prayer that I circled the issue in the first paragraph before identifying it in the second.

God, I'm tempted to cash in my chips today. I just want to quit everything and go off somewhere alone. I feel like I'm running hard to nowhere. I want out from under it all. I started too young. I got lots of strokes for being so far along for my age. Now age has caught up with me. I'm taken for granted. God, it's lonely at the top of whatever heap I'm on. What's the use? Why spend my life doing this? Surely there is more to life than listening to people complain about budgets and offerings and orders of worship. Where is the sacred part of my life—the part that nobody attacks or hurts, the part that is vulnerable to no one and no thing? I am naked and exposed. There is no protection. I'm tired of being considered so strong, as if I had no feelings.

I have been betrayed, not by accident, not by uncontrollable circumstances, but by willful intent. God, this hurts in a strange way. I guess this is what I want to talk to you about. It's all expressed to me in a "you'll understand and accept this" kind of way. I ought to want to lash out, get even, hurt back, destroy, make Jack pay, but I feel none of these. Maybe I'm too numb to feel anything. I don't like the notion, "He'll get over this and everything will be OK." I feel bitter, and I sense I'm slipping into despair, even apathy. How can this be happening to me? I've been kidding myself. The fool at the party is me. I've been used. I've been lied to. I feel laughed at, spit on, stepped on, kicked.

I guess I'm moralizing now, God, but I think I know how you feel when I betray you. Yet, following those times I have never felt unwanted or unloved by you. That is a warm, supportive surprise. On the one hand I want to be loving and accepting toward Jack, my betrayer. On the other hand, I don't want to run the risk of being betrayed again. What guarantees do I have? What guarantees do you have about my trustworthiness? God, help me forgive Jack. Please forgive me for betraying you. Amen.

Antagonist. An antagonist is one whose attitude or state of mind is in active opposition to a person or issue. The antagonistic enemy is obvious, perhaps even blatant, in his opposition. His facial expressions and voice inflections convey his antagonism. It may be that many things have gone awry in his life and for some reason those are collectively focused on me. The positive thing about the antagonist is that I know where he stands—directly opposite of me. He may not know what he wants until I express myself, and then he is certain he does not want that.

Often the antagonist is a trap setter. He asks questions to which he already knows the answers, at least the answers he wants. He hopes to be able to say, in his mind at least, in hearing my answer, "Now I gotcha."

On more than one occasion, the Pharisees attempted to trap Jesus with their questions. They expected either/or answers. Jesus surprised them every time with at least a third alternative. It is significant that Jesus was more like the Pharisees than any of the religious leaders of his day. Yet, they were his antagonists.

Knowing what the antagonist's position is makes praying for him more difficult because then the situation seems hopeless. More accurately, I feel helpless rather than the situation being hopeless. Admitting my helplessness aids me in realizing that I cannot do everything. Then I am freed to discover there are some things I can do.

Father,

I don't know what to do about it—it all seems so useless. Before I even get the first sentence of the sermon out of my mouth, Roseanne is squirming and fidgeting. That grin on her face is so forced. It seems to be covering animosity and hostility. I used to think Roseanne had become like this only in recent years, but some of her conversations lately indicate that she has always disliked me. It is painful and difficult for me to discover and admit that someone really despises me.

Being able to say all of this to you, Father, seems to help. I don't feel antagonistic toward her. I can't identify any secret desire to get back at her. Sometimes I go out of my way to speak to Roseanne and to be friendly just because I think she is avoiding me. I am amazed at how calm I can be with her. Thank you, Father, for helping me to do that. God help Roseanne to get that antagonistic poison out of her system. She is destroying herself, and I don't want her to do that. Is there any way we can reach Roseanne? Can she be saved? Amen.

Learning to pray begins with ourselves but very quickly expands to include praying for friends and enemies. The key for me in petitionary prayer is the discovery that it involves the psychology of communication rather than the psychology of will. To live a life of prayer means to be open-eyed to myself and to see my neediness, brokenness, and godlessness and to see others and the world as they are. Prayer forms my existence. A life formed by prayer is one formed by the sober truth. Pretense is no longer necessary because it is no longer worth the trouble.

What I have discovered in praying for friends and enemies is that there is nothing human that is alien to me. My friends and my enemies are my brothers and sisters. If I address my godlessness to God, I cannot be thankful that I am not like others. I can only plead, "Lord, be merciful to me, a sinner." The result of this is solidarity formed with my friends and enemies. In praying for them, I identify with their joys, pain, brokenness, and godlessness. If this is my prayer, then I cannot live in contradiction with this prayer by fleeing my friends and enemies. Praying for friends and enemies develops solidarity rather than isolation. I will always have both friends and enemies. Learning to pray for them is valuable for me.

Notes

1. George S. Hendry, "The Life Line of Theology," *The Princeton Seminary Bulletin 65*, 1972, pp. 22-30.

2. Paul E. Johnson, *Psychology of Religion* (New York: Abingdon Press, 1959), p. 132.

3. David Elkind, "The Child's Conception of Prayer," *The Child's Reality: Three Developmental Themes* (Hillsdale, N.J.: Laurence Erlbaum Associates, 1978), pp. 27-45.

4. Donald Capps, "The Psychology of Petitionary Prayer," *Theology Today*, Vol. XXXIX, No. 2, pp. 130-141.

5. Theodore Newcomb, "An Approach to the Study of Communication," *Psychological Review 60* (1953), pp. 392-403.

4

Learning to Pray for the Sick

Is anyone among you suffering? Let him pray. Is any cheerful? Let him sing praise. Is any among you sick? Let him call for the elders of the church and let them pray over him, anointing him with oil in the name of the Lord; and the prayer of faith will save the sick man, and the Lord will raise him up; and if he has committed sins, he will be forgiven.

Therefore confess your sins to one another, and pray for one another, that you may be healed. The prayer of a righteous man has great power in its effects (Jas. 5:13-16).

Hardly a day goes by that someone doesn't ask me to pray for him. Often these prayer requests are for the sick. Although each person's illness or hospitalization is unique in its impact upon the individual, there are some common dynamics among the sick, regardless of the nature of their debilitation. I want to identify some of the issues that affect persons who are incapacitated because of illness or accident and demonstrate that praying for the sick and injured reflects their needs. Included are prayers I have written for the sick and injured.

Issues for the Sick

Nature of the Illness

Three important questions are on the mind of anyone who is incapacitated: (1) what is wrong with me? (2) what are the chances for my recovery? and (3) what will be involved in my recovery from this illness? These questions are related to diagnosis, prognosis, and treatment. One concern that parallels diagnosis is the cause. The diagnostic process may involve only a brief appointment with a physician, or it may require hospitalization and numerous tests conducted over several days or weeks to determine the nature of the illness.

The treatment procedures run the gamut of options from diet or medication to radical surgery. Naturally, the more involved the treatment, the more intense is the physical and emotional energy expended by the patient in coping with the illness.

Reactions to the Illness

The number and intensity of reactions to illness may be as varied as the people who are ill; however, there are some reactions common to those who are sick, regardless of the cause.

Fear. The first reaction is fear and is expressed in the diagnostic question, What is wrong with me? When one becomes ill and before the exact problem is identified, anxiety is present. The concern not only is what is wrong with me? but also how will whatever is wrong with me affect me in the future? This fear is a natural response to what is occurring in the person's life and in no way is an indication of a lack of confidence in God. This fear affects the deeply committed worshiper of God and the one who claims neither interest nor belief in God. The greatest fear any of us experiences is the fear of the unknown.

Death is the greatest unknown for all of us. Because it is impossible to die and live to tell about it, no one can bring us a message from the great unknown that will dissipate our fears. Paul Tillich has identified well this fear. "The anxiety of death overshadows all concrete anxieties and gives them their ultimate seriousness."[1]

Once a correct diagnosis has been made, a sense of relief is often experienced. There is some comfort in knowing what is wrong and in eliminating all the things that one imagined might be wrong. In situations where I have become overly concerned with all the things that might be wrong, I have found this statement, attributed to various people, helpful. "I am an old man and have known many troubles, but most of them never happened."

Correct diagnosis does not alleviate all fear. Betty was fifty-two when first diagnosed with cancer. Surgery was performed and all malignancy removed. Two years later the cancer reappeared and spread rapidly. While I was visiting Betty, she expressed some of her fears.

I don't know what is going to happen. I don't want to upset

Tom. I don't know whether to take chemotherapy. It made me so sick last time. I wish I could gain some strength. Maybe then I could go home. I don't want to be a burden on anyone. I guess I'm not really afraid to die, but I am afraid of what all will happen before I die.

Control. Related to fear of the unknown is the issue of control. All of us want to be in control of ourselves. Being sick means something is happening that we cannot control, and we cannot know what effect it will have on us. Persons facing surgery often relate their control concerns to being anesthetized. Richard Blancher suggests that, for many people, the anesthesia may be more frightening than the surgery since it is equated with dying, forced passivity, or loss of control.[2] Comments by two persons regarding anesthesia support the control question as an issue. One patient said, "I want to know what is going on," and another said, "I don't like to be groggy so that I'm not at all myself." Part of what is occurring intrapersonally when someone is out of control is the threat of losing oneself.

Probably the most common indicator of loss of control for those who are sick is crying. The tears may well up in the person's eyes or flow uncontrollably. Usually the person is apologetic and embarrassed at the loss of control. Understanding and affirming the expression of feelings is vital. If I am uneasy at the time of the patient's loss of control, I probably will hamper the relationship and cause the patient to turn his feelings inward, deny their existence, or conclude that there are some feelings that are not permitted to be expressed to me. Many believe there are feelings that are not to be shared with anyone or with God. This attitude is part of a person's denial mechanism.

Dependency. Tension is felt by the person who is sick because he is dependent on another to care for some or all of his needs. Even those who enjoy being waited on "hand and foot" struggle with the issue of dependency. Here is where control and dependency are closely related because many of us want to be in control of how dependent we are on others. Self-worth becomes a concern because we partially define our value as persons on the basis of our ability to do things for ourselves. It is with internal struggle that the sick permit others to help them.

Whenever a person gets sick, seldom is there just one issue raised by the illness. The patient's needs are compounded by fear, control, dependency, and concern for family members. As a church member prepared for surgery, she raised many concerns which I collected in the following prayer.

Father,

Mary is burdened. She is facing surgery that she says is no more involved than having crowns put on teeth. That's no big deal when it is someone else's teeth. In some ways, the surgery is the least of her concerns. She is wondering whether John will receive proper care while she is away and whether Joe and Sue will get along with each other. Almost every day she sees John losing ground to his illness. Mary is very sad.

Next week, at least for a couple of days following the surgery, Mary will be virtually helpless. It is very difficult for her to depend on anyone or to ask for help. Father, free her from her independent compulsion enough to seek and accept the assistance others can give.

Father, the load for Mary is heavy. Assure her of your presence. Make her aware that she is not alone but that you are traveling with her every moment, offering her strength and sustenance for the living of these days. Amen.

Anger. A prevalent emotional reaction to illness is anger. After all, the regular routine of life is interrupted. Plans have to be rearranged. Work time is lost. Completing personal projects is delayed. The expenses of the illness deplete financial resources. All of this seems grossly unfair. Anger is a natural response to illness and often is expressed in the question, Why did this happen to me? No satisfactory answer is possible for this question because it is a speculative question. Regardless of what answer is given, it probably will only cause one to expand the why question. Attempting to answer why is a dead-end street, but identifying the anger one has about one's situation is a needed step in adjusting to what has happened.

Naming the feeling to God is a helpful way to constructively deal with anger. To name anything is to have some control over it. A person must deal with feelings or feelings deal with the person. Anger in response to illness results from feeling unfairly treated. The real agony is, How do I go on living now that this has happened to me? Learning to pray for the sick involves naming to God the anger one feels for what is happening to the person who is sick.

Body Awareness. The biblical view of humanity is that a person is a living being. A person does not have a soul; a person is a soul. What happens in one aspect of life affects the other areas of life. Physical illness affects one's emotional well-being and may cause her to reexamine her religious commitments and her view of God. A person's identity is tied directly to her awareness of her body. The body, its appearance and function, is crucial to self-esteem, and a person struggles to integrate a new body status, altered by illness or surgery, into her self-concept.

Injury caused by accident also affects body awareness. Injury may affect appearance as well as function. These reminders of the injury and of the events surrounding the accident cause one to continue reliving the accident and may cause one to project dislike for self because of body awareness. Of course, if this dislike becomes self-hatred, it can be self-destructive. Attempted and accomplished suicides are among the expressions of dislike for the person one is. Many factors contribute to this negative body awareness. The following prayer voices my concern for one who attempted suicide and my pain in being unable to reach her.

Father,
I don't know what happened to Melissa. Oh, I know she took too many sleeping pills, mixed with another drug, but I really don't know what happened. What consumed her? Was it loneliness? Whom did she need to touch her? Was it I, Lord?
I know Melissa is trying to self-destruct. I don't want her to do that. I am thankful she is still alive. I hope there is no lasting physical damage. No doubt there will be some emotional scars. Maybe she feels like a failure, and now her attempted suicide is just another failure. Oh, God, I want her to get well. I want her life to be fulfilling. She is just too young to end it all.

Lord, I know you like Melissa, but she doesn't like herself. I see her screaming for help, but I can't seem to reach her. The line is disconnected. I feel like she is drowning in a sea of loneliness, swept along by the waves of low self-esteem and caught by the undertow of anger.

Most of the time Melissa hates her father. She would like to love him and have him love her, but it doesn't happen. Maybe it's too late for that. I hope not, but if it is, can some of us love her enough to bring her back from the brink? Can we love her long enough and deep enough to help her get well? God, I know this is what you want for Melissa. Help her, Lord, to want life more than death.

God, relieve Melissa of her self-destructive anger, deliver her from her loneliness, fill her with your love and acceptance. Help us to love and accept her. Help us to reach her, Lord. Help us to connect. Amen.

Guilt and Punishment. The ability to think, to reason, is a tremendous gift. A person's reasoning ability can be a terrible plague if he begins viewing what is happening to him as punishment for a wrong he has committed. No one lives for very long without doing something wrong. Guilt is an emotional response to having done something wrong. Illness, surgery, or an accident often surfaces those feelings of guilt and compounds the struggle a person is having. Many of us attempt to deal with our guilt all by ourselves. Since we cannot get ourselves off our hands, we conclude that our hardship is punishment for our wrongs. That is a terrible feeling to put on oneself. It is even worse to have friends impose such a judgment as Job's friends did.

As we are learning to pray for the sick, we need to listen to their hints of guilt and punishment. When there is an indication of being punished, it is helpful to ask for what they are being punished and how what is happening to them fits the wrong they committed. Several years ago I met a woman who was overloaded with guilt from the death of an eighteen-month-old son four years previously. She said, "It was all my fault!" She seemed to believe that the reason she needed a hysterectomy was because she was being punished for being an irresponsible mother.

The day I wrote this I visited a man in the hospital who in the last six years has undergone three major surgeries. He suffers from angina and severe emphysema which requires frequent oxygen use. He is hospitalized now because of a broken leg resulting from a blackout and a fall. He said to me, "I don't know what I have done to deserve all of this. I don't think I could possibly have been so bad to deserve this." I agreed with him that there was no correlation between how he has lived and the multitude of health problems he has experienced. Before leaving him, I prayed:

> Father,
> You know the long and difficult struggles George has had the last six years. There are days when all that has happened to him overwhelms and inundates him so that he feels immobile in mind and body. Some days these feelings lead to despair.
> Today the despair has degenerated into guilt. Lord, George wonders if he's being punished, but he knows you don't work like that. He just can't comprehend why all of this happened to him. Neither can I. We know there is no satisfactory answer to, why? I know you are not doling out punishment to George through all of these health problems. Help him to know that too. Help him find renewed courage for today through his awareness of your love for him. Help him realize that you are his companion in this lonely valley of struggle and suffering. We pray in the name of One who knew struggle and suffering, Jesus Christ our Lord. Amen.

Neededness. Illness often strikes a person's self-worth with gale force winds, causing him to feel useless and worthless. One of the most vulnerable areas in the life of one imprisoned by illness is neededness. Every person needs to be needed. When one is sick she sees more readily that others continue to function even though she is incapacitated. The family gets through the day-to-day routine. The place of her employment continues to be open for business. *No one is indispensable. Maybe nobody needs me anymore,* are the types of thoughts occupying much of the patient's thinking. Learning to pray for the sick includes awareness of the sick person's need to be needed. It is helpful when dialoguing with the sick to identify what contributions they are making to me. To identify those contributions to the person and to express gratitude for those contributions when praying for the sick will affirm the person's worth and neededness. The following prayer illustrates what I am suggesting:

> Thank you, Father, for this time Bill and I have had to visit together. The bond of our friendship is strengthened each time we are together. Bill is teaching me much about living and dying. He is so candid about what is happening to him. God, there seems to be such a thin line between the inevitability of death and the desire to live. Bill seems to be able to walk that line. I hope I can learn to walk that line, too. Bill is teaching me how. Thank you, Father, for helping Bill to be my teacher. Amen.

Location of the Patient. Bondage comes in many forms. Illness is one. It is a bondage whether the confinement results from disease, surgery, or accident. The person in bondage may find hope in the promise of God to the Israelites:

> Then the Lord said, "I have seen the affliction of my people who are in Egypt and have heard their cry because of their taskmasters; I know their sufferings, and I have come down to deliver them out of the hand of the Egyptians" (Ex. 3:7-8).

A person who already is caught in the bondage of illness may resign from all activity until he is well again. This trap must be avoided, and a helpful question to ask in this regard is, What are you going to do while you're waiting to be freed from the bondage of illness?

Jeremiah asked a similar question of God, concerning his people who were in Exile. Here is the answer Jeremiah received and gave to those in bondage.

> Build houses and live in them; plant gardens and eat their produce. Take wives and have sons and daughters; take wives for your sons, and give your daughters in marriage, that they may bear sons and daughters; multiply there, and do not decrease. But seek the welfare of the city

where I have sent you into exile, and pray to the Lord on its behalf, for in
its welfare you will find your welfare (Jer. 29:5-7).

Where a person is located while he is sick has an impact on his
attitude and well-being. As long as the sick can be cared for at home,
that usually is where they prefer to be, and why not? Home is their usual
habitat, with familiar surroundings. A person feels he is a little more in
control of his situation when he is at home. Naturally, there are
occasions when hospitalization is necessary. In other situations, the sick
will need to go to the home of a family member, a hospice center, or a
nursing home. The ability to be at ease in any of these away from home
places corresponds largely to the concern and interest demonstrated by
those responsible for the patient's care. Also affecting the sick will be
their attitudes about their situations, what their needs are, if and how
those needs are being met.

Whether the sick person's needs are being met also becomes the
concern of family members and friends. The person who is sick may be
the identified patient, but in actuality the entire family is affected and in
need of care. This probably is most evident when a child is hospitalized.
I really cannot pray for the sick without praying for the others in the
family.

Father,
    Truly you are the eternal lover of children. You know how
frightening it is for Angela to be in the hospital. All of those
strangers dressed in their unfamiliar white outfits add to the fright.
When her parents must leave, her fear increases. *What if they
don't return?* she wonders. Calm Angela's fears. Assure her that
her parents will return. Help her to know that these white-suited
strangers are her friends.
    Angela's parents are concerned, too, Lord. Perhaps their minds
are their own worst enemies. How many times today have they
asked, What if . . . ? What if she doesn't get better? What if the
bronchial infection leads to pneumonia? Reduce their anxieties
and calm the storm of fear in their lives. May they have confidence
that you are journeying beside them through every anxious
moment.

Ronald is troubled too. He wants his sister to be well and home again. He wonders what is happening to her. *Will she be OK? When?* Calm Ronald's anxiousness and assure him of your care for him and for Angela.

Thank you, Father, for Angela's doctors and for the hospital staff who care for her. Thank you for people who are doing all they can to help her get well. Thank you for giving them the insight, comprehension, and sensitivity to work for Angela's well-being. May the sterile odors and the frightful feelings soon pass away. May Angela soon be well and at home again. Amen.

Illness Association. When a person becomes ill, she often associates her illness with a previous illness, either hers or that of a significant person in her life. Whether her illness is similar or not even remotely related to the previous one, her tendency is to conclude that whatever happened then will be repeated now. One of the needs of the sick is to deal with the anxiety that memory raises. The following prayer is an example of my attempt to do this in praying for William.

Father,

This is a tough day for William. He returns to the hospital. This time he is the patient. Last time it was Frances. The cancer multiplied so rapidly, quickly and quietly choking out her life. As William drove up to the hospital, a hundred flashbacks must have whizzed through his mind.

The doctor has assured William that his tumor is benign. He believes him—he has believed him for nine months. Yet, there is a question, a doubt. Will this surgery be a success? Will I survive? What will I be like if I survive? There are William's fears, Lord. Calm the storm that fear brings.

Surgery is only part of the journey. Recuperation takes a long time. Hours pass like days in the hospital. Many times in the loneliness of this journey, William will look up at the ceiling and ask, How long? How long? Give William the courage to cope with the pain he experiences. Lord, assure William that no matter how long, you will be his constant companion and faithful friend. May William know that his help and hope rest in you. Amen.

Learning to pray for the sick involves empathy, attempting to put oneself in another's place. I need to be careful, however, in overstating my ability to understand what the illness is like for the person. A safeguard for me is to ask myself, How do I know what this is like for the patient? When I cannot answer that, I need to be honest enough not to claim more understanding than I have. The person will perceive my phoniness if I make a grandiose claim although he may kindly not confront me. The following prayer for Cathy was an attempt to express what I understood to be her needs, held in the tension of not claiming more than I understood.

Father,

Cathy has had a very frightening experience. I have no idea what it would be like to be run over by a car, but I know just the thought of it causes me to feel panicky and to break out in a cold sweat. Perhaps the flashbacks of the accident are as troublesome to Cathy's mind as anything.

Of course there have been the why questions: Why did this happen? Why was I in the path of the car? Why wasn't I more careful? Father, for every answer to a why question, why are there three more whys? Maybe Cathy is angry that this happened to her. I am. I wish the accident hadn't happened. I wish no one ever had to go through this kind of tragedy.

Mixed with all of these fears and wishes is the pain, the incessant, excruciating pain that sometimes comes with every breath and certainly with every move. God, help Cathy to cope with the pain. Continue to work with her and the medical staff to bring about healing.

Lord, as the healing process continues, a new fear arises. Now there is the fear of therapy. Cathy doesn't want to make any move that will hurt, and yet she must. She doesn't want to fall, and yet to be able to walk she will have to take that risk. Oh, Father, help Cathy to know that you are moving with her every move, that you are walking with her every step, and that you are crying with her every pain.

Father, I am grateful that Cathy is alive. I am grateful that you have made her body so that it can be healed. I am certain that this entire experience will make an indelible mark on Cathy's life. I trust that the mark will be one of gratitude for life rather than bitterness or resentment. Continue to hold Cathy in your arms, give her comfort and peace today and every day in this long journey from brokenness to wholeness. Amen.

Praying for the Sick

Having written about the issues that are alive for the sick and shared prayers expressing some of these concerns, I briefly want to identify some guidelines I have found helpful in learning to pray for the sick.

Praying for the sick involves much more than cloaking some concern in God talk. The temptation seems to be present with me always to use vain repetitions in praying for the sick. Jesus said, "And in praying do not heap up empty phrases as the Gentiles do; for they think that they will be heard for their many words" (Matt. 6:7).

Listen with Interest

Listening is a significant part of communicating. Learning to pray for anyone, including the sick, is to communicate with God what is in the best interest of those for whom I pray. Listening with interest to the sick will enable me to hear many of their needs. As a means of verbalizing anger and unfairness, they may be asking the speculative question, Why? Certainly the sick need someone who will listen to them tell what it is like to be afraid, angry, isolated, out of control, needy, or guilty. Part of listening also is questioning. Does the person want me to pray with him or for him, or neither? The patient's psychic space needs to be respected. It is helpful to the patient and to me to ask if he wants me to pray for him. Another thing I need to know is for what the patient wants me to pray. This is a way of asking a person what one needs in a manner that often is easier for one to respond. I may easily and unconsciously transfer to the patient what I think his needs are and pray for something that really is not the concern of the patient. There is the story of the mother who was eager to clue into her son's sexual questions as soon as they arose. She kept her antennae out for any noise in this area. The opportunity came one day where her son asked, "Mommy, how did I get here?" Well, she made the most of the opportunity and told him about things she had been afraid to ask, as well as things she had never thought of asking when she was younger. When she finished, her son look extremely puzzled. Having been told that they had moved from another city when he was a baby, he asked, "I mean, did we come by train or by airplane?" In having my antennae out for any noise in the area of fear that one who is sick may have, I may miss what his more pressing concern is.

Asking the right question is helpful. Mark's Gospel records the encounter of Bartimaeus with Jesus (Mark 10:46-52). During that dialogue, Jesus asked a very significant question, "What do you want me to do for you?" In learning to pray for the sick, it is very helpful to ask two questions: (1) Do you want me to pray for you? and (2) For what do you want me to pray? In my visit with Betty, I asked those questions, and her answer to the second question was a surprise. I had anticipated she would want me to pray for her to get well or to pray for her family, but her request was that I pray for her to have the strength she needed to endure her illness and whatever might be involved in the illness. She had some fear of the unknown and felt her need was to have the stamina to journey through that unknown. Here is my prayer.

> Lord, the richest promise you have made is your promise to be with us in whatever we face. Today, more than ever, we need to experience the truth of that promise. In a sense, Father, the conversation that Betty and I have been having is our prayer. You have heard her many concerns. The main thing Betty needs, Lord, is strength. She doesn't know all that is going to happen to her because of cancer. As a matter of fact, she doesn't know anything for certain about what will happen. But she needs the fortitude, the courage, the confidence to journey through the days ahead with meaning and purpose. Her confidence and hope are in you, Father. May she receive strength and encouragement from you. Amen.

Ironically, when I ask the sick for what they want me to pray, the requests generally are for strength, courage, endurance, comfort, and the ability to cope rather than a request to get well or to experience a miracle in the sense of a suspension of the natural order or to receive some special dispensation from God that others do not receive. The requests for special favors from God often come from family members and friends rather than from the sick themselves.

Of course, all praying does not have to be verbalized. There are situations when verbal prayer is an intrusion, such as when family members or friends are present and verbal prayer might reveal some intimate or confidential needs the patient is not ready to share with others. Prayer and the sharing of prayer concerns is not to serve as the church's grapevine for information.

George Buttrick, a great Presbyterian preacher, at age eighty-four was still writing a sermon a week "whether I need it or not."[3] There is value in writing a prayer a day, whether I need it or not. I have discovered the value of writing prayers for the sick. Writing a prayer helps me formulate my concerns. Over a period of time the written prayers serve as a spiritual journal. To write a prayer for a specific person enables me to focus on that person, and then when I talk with him I am better able to listen with interest.

Speak with Integrity

A potential hazard in asking for what one wants me to pray is the request I cannot honor. Two examples occurred recently—one was a request from a woman that I pray for her son who had committed suicide two weeks earlier. The other was a request that I offer a prayer of thanksgiving to God for keeping an individual from having an automobile accident in a near-miss situation. If he kept this individual from having an accident, why doesn't he keep everyone accident free? I am becoming better able to express to persons why I cannot pray for some things because of what such prayers imply about God.

Prayer must not be used as a denial mechanism. People declare that if the sick will just pray, they will get well. In this way, prayer is used as a shield against the disease to keep the persons from facing the difficult reality and often inevitable consequences of their situations. Prayer may become a way to avoid talking about life and death issues.

To speak with integrity regarding prayer also involves honesty about what prayer is and what it does. We must be careful about promising more than prayer can deliver. For many people, a very thin division exists between religion and magic, especially where prayer is concerned.

Often recovery from illness is attributed to prayer, but when recovery does not occur for others who had prayed for the same thing, a fail-safe response about prayer is given. Either no comment is made about such situations or it is said that people did not pray in the right way or it was not God's will. This fail-safe approach for prayer lacks integrity and adds guilt to the devastation already felt by the sick.

View of God

When learning to pray for the sick, keep in mind that God always is on the side of health and wholeness. It is only right that we be on the side of health and well-being as we commune with God about our desire for those who are exiled to the bondage of illness and who want to be set free and made whole again. We need also to be aware that God does not want any person to be sick or injured, but in order to create us as free persons in a free universe, he limited himself. In this sense God can't do everything, but he can do many things. If we are really serious about praying for the sick, then our praying must involve a willingness to put some of our energy at God's disposal for him to use, if possible. Genuine intercessory prayer involves me in being a partner with God for the benefit of whomever I pray. Otherwise, my prayers are as a clanging cymbal or a noisy gong signifying nothing.

The Scripture passage quoted at the beginning of this chapter suggests that prayer or communion with God ought to bracket life. Both when hardship brings discouragement and when life goes smoothly and one is cheerful, one ought to pray to God. Are not these extremes the brackets of life, and is not sickness a time of weakness in life? In all these situations, an individual is to pray. When the sick are too weak to pray for themselves, those in the church are to pray for them. It was the practice in the Jewish community for the village elders to visit the dangerously ill and pray with them. If the ill were too weak to pray, the elders prayed on their behalf while those who were sick prayed "in their hearts."

Learning to pray for the sick is an enlarging and sensitizing experience. It makes me more aware of the universality of the bondage of disease and injury and more aware of a loving God who is always on the side of health and wholeness. Learning to pray for the sick begins to tear down the wall of selfishness and to construct a bridge of empathy. In a significant way, when I pray for the sick, I also pray for myself, resulting in enlarged vision and enlarged love for fellow human beings.

Notes

1. Paul Tillich, *The Courage to Be* (New Haven: Yale University Press, 1952), p. 43.

2. Richard S. Blacher, "Loss of Internal Organ," *Loss and Grief: Psychological Management in Medical Practice*, ed. Bernard Schonberg (New York: W. W. Norton & Co., Inc., 1970), p. 137.

3. Stated in preaching class, Louisville Presbyterian Seminary, Louisville, Kentucky, 1972.

5

Learning to Pray
for the Grief Sufferer

I am weary with my moaning;
 every night I flood my bed with tears;
 I drench my couch with my weeping.
My eye wastes away because of grief,
 it grows weak because of all my foes (Ps. 6:6-7).

No one lives long before becoming "a person of sorrows acquainted with grief." Human death is the most traumatic cause of grief; but there are other "deaths" in life that cause grief reactions. Grief is a universal experience. An examination of what grief is, an explanation of what grief does, and an identification of who some of the grievers are will contribute to learning to pray for the grief sufferer.

What Grief Is

Grief is the emotional reaction to a significant loss in life that results from being separated from a person or place of significance. How deeply one feels the loss is in correlation to the attachment one has to the person or place from which one is separated. Grief is a tearing, emotional response because the loss shuts off the griever from the fulfillment of hopes, dreams, and aspirations.

There are many crises that evoke grief reactions. A crisis is any event or set of circumstances that interrupts a person's normal routine or pattern of living and threatens one's sense of well-being or existence.

One of the aspects of the grief dynamic is its personalization. Part of what evokes an emotionally upsetting reaction to loss is the awareness of finitude. The griever personalizes what has occurred and says, "That could happen to me." Just a few months ago I heard about the death of a news commentator. I had heard him report the news on the radio, but had never met him. News of his death jolted me when the reporter said that the deceased was thirty-four years old—my age.

Grief reactions do not discriminate against sex, race, or class. The very young and the very old grieve because of loss, as do men, women, red, yellow, black and white, rich and poor. For many children, their first grief experience is the death of a pet. The emotional trauma is present with them although they may have difficulty verbalizing it.

During my twelfth year, I was awakened one morning by my mother's voice. She was talking on the telephone. Then I heard the telephone being dialed and overheard my father's voice. I knew something traumatic had happened. I hesitated getting up because of the struggle between wanting and not wanting to know what had happened. As I listened to one side of more conversations, I knew one of my grand-fathers had died. This discovery made me more reluctant to get up as the internal tug-of-war intensified. When I finally did get up, my parents told me that my paternal grandfather had died. I felt embedded in the couch where I was sitting. At that time, that grandfather was the most significant person I had known who had died. I could not move. Soon it was breakfast time, but I had no appetite. I went to school and was surprised that my teacher already had heard the news. Later that day and other days I was hungry, but when the food was prepared, one or two bites were sufficient. Rest and sleep were difficult. Euphoria and despair seemed to chase each other through my body, as my mind raced to recall encounters with my grandfather. I felt "washed out," and my face had a worn and haggard appearance.

What Grief Does

In addition to defining grief, I also have identified some of the emotional and physical symptoms of grief. You may have had similar symptoms, as well as emotional ones such as sighing, emptiness, and speechlessness. These grief symptoms reveal something of what grief does.

The grief process begins at the time a person becomes aware of a loss and continues until one has assimilated the meaning of the loss into life and readjusted to a normal pattern of living. It is a process because it involves changes and movements, but not in a smooth, steady, clearly defined progression. Rather, the process is like a chord progression on the piano. In going from one chord to another, notes may be included in a second chord that were in the first; yet the sound and impression are different and indicate harmonic movements.

The grief process involves a back and forth movement from one step to another. The backward movement is never all the way back to zero, although the griever often feels that it is. One may say, "I thought I was adjusting OK until yesterday. I feel like I did when this first happened." The fact that the griever can talk with some objectivity about the process is an indication that the backward movement is not back to "square one."

A wealth of material has been published in recent years concerning grief. Differing lists of the stages of grief have been compiled ranging from Cassem's two stages[1] to Westberg's ten stages.[2] I list six stages of grief.

Shock. When I answered the telephone last fall, there was a pause. Then I heard a woman's voice I did not recognize. She sobbed, "Howard, the store burned last night." I wondered *What store? Where?* Then I recognized the voice of my mother and realized that the store was one my parents owned. Mother was shocked by the loss.

Persons who have received the news of the death of a family member or close friend often express feelings like they have a huge weight on their chests, like being in a daze, or they want to think but their minds won't function. These and other reactions are symptoms of shock. The shock waves serve as a type of emotional anesthesia to deaden some of the pain for the griever for a season.

Numbness. When the shock wears off, the griever is left numb. In the case of a death, this often is how family members and close friends feel at the time of a funeral. Numbness doesn't mean that they feel nothing, but rather that their emotions are distorted, their reaction time is slowed, and their thinking capacity is foggy. Part of the cause of the numbness is the extreme emotions they have experienced. They are worn out from the flood of feelings that has roared through their lives as their memory has caused laughter and crying. They have relived and retold the "death event" many times, and each time much emotional energy has been spent.

The pain of loss is intense, and the griever often wishes he had died in place of the deceased. He seems convinced that would have been easier and better. This was David's attitude at the death of Absalom.

> And the king was deeply moved, and went up to the chamber over the gate, and wept; and as he went, he said, "O my son Absalom, my son, my son Absalom! Would I had died instead of you, O Absalom, my son, my son!" (2 Sam. 18:33).

Fantasy. Whatever the death is, loss of job, a child leaving home, or death of a spouse, part of the process of adjusting to the loss is fantasizing about the situation being different than it is. Some people pretend that the loss didn't happen. Many people in Western cultures work overtime emotionally in denying the pain they feel because of loss. Serious problems develop if a person refuses to face reality and uses fantasy as a method of denial. Generally, what happens is that a griever fantasizes about one who has died and then some event or some word from another person brings the griever back to reality. It is not uncommon for a griever to say to himself, "Oh, I want to tell Mary about that," and then he realizes that Mary is dead and he can't tell her.

I knew a woman who on more than one occasion prepared dinner, set the table for two, and then when it came time for her husband to come in, realized he wouldn't be coming. He had died several weeks earlier. This was very disconcerting for her. She was fearful she was losing her mind. Reactions such as this one are part of the emotional reflex caused by grief.

Depression. A concise and popular definition of emotional depression is anger turned inward. Two very strong emotions unleashed because of death or loss are hostility and guilt. Actually, these two feelings are like two sides of the same coin.

Hostility is a natural response to any crisis. We often are angry when some unexpected or even an anticipated event upsets our normal patterns of living. Were a person to lose his job, it would be natural for him to be angry at the employer or at the economic situation that forced his unemployment. It is not unusual for the anger to be misdirected, either turned in on oneself or taken out on a family member. It is my observation that when unemployment in this country rises, so do spouse and child abuse.

Misdirected anger was illustrated in a recent cartoon. A man has a very difficult day at work and arrives home frustrated. His wife speaks to him and he yells at her. She turns and screams at the older child, who then screams at his younger sister. The younger sister then kicks the dog and the caption reads, "It would have been better for the man to have kicked the dog."

When an accident happens or a death occurs, it may not be easy either to identify or focus the anger. The anger usually is expressed in the speculative question, Why did this happen? A teenager recuperating from an accident that will leave scars for the rest of her life was asking "Why?" I inquired at whom she was angry, and she responded immediately that she was angry at God for permitting such an accident to happen. From her perspective, other people had taken the same chances she had and came away unharmed.

Guilt could be identified as anger at oneself either for failing to take a certain action or for taking action that contributed to or caused the loss. Loss often is followed by second-guessing, and such second-guessing usually is prefaced by *if*. Implied in the *if* expression is that one event done differently would have altered the entire outcome of the situation for the better.

Stabbing Pain. As a person journeys through the grief process, there are events, sights, and sounds that remind her of the loss. A person adjusting to divorce sees someone who reminds her of her former spouse. There is a rush of feelings through her body as she is reminded of what she has lost. A song is played on the radio that has been heard many times before, but this time the words convey reminders of an important person who has moved away, is estranged, or has died. Anniversaries, birthdays, and holidays also may be reminders. Whatever the reminder, the griever relives the loss experience in miniature.

Readjustment. People often comment that time heals, but time has no healing power. The events that occur with the passing of time can help the griever to integrate the meaning of the loss into his life.

One of the concerns grievers have is how long it will take for life to get back to normal. They are aware that life will never be like it was before the loss occurred, but they want to arrive at the point where all of life is not revolving around the loss. Generally, the grief process takes twelve to eighteen months for the griever to move from the initial shock to a readjustment and resumption of normal living patterns. Of course, the nature of the loss and the constitution of the griever affect the intensity and longevity of the process.

It is not uncommon for a griever to become stuck at some stage in the grief process. It is helpful for every griever to have an objective person with whom he can talk out his feelings about his loss. This is especially necessary when one gets stuck somewhere in the process. Often the presenting problem appears to have nothing to do with the loss the person has experienced. A young woman made an appointment to see me. Early in the first interview, she indicated she was having trouble sleeping. When she did sleep, she had nightmares about catastrophic endings of the world. Her fear of the world ending was immobilizing her emotionally. Her father had died about two months earlier. As I was able to get her to talk about her feelings concerning her loss of him, the emotional blockage began to break up. She talked about what life would be like without her dad. As she named her fears, she began to be able to deal with them and soon continued the process of grieving. Eventually she was able to readjust to her normal living pattern.

Because grief is a natural, emotional response to loss, there are some indicators of abnormal grieving. Being alert to some of these indicators not only will facilitate the ability to pray for the griever but also may enable one to get the griever the kind of help needed. A clear sign of abnormal grieving is the total absence of grief in the face of a loss. This approach may be caused by the fear that feelings will get out of control or the idea that to deny that loss has occurred means it has not happened. Additional signs of abnormal grieving or refusal to grieve include overactivity, suspicious hostility toward specific persons, suppressed hostility, self-destructive behavior, such as selling all of one's possessions, heavy dependence on drugs and alcohol, or serious insomnia. Other indicators are increasing withdrawal and social isolation and persistent one-sided descriptions of the situation or the person who died.

The causes of grief are multiple. Some of the more common causes are: death, altered body image resulting from surgery, divorce, death of a pet, a child leaving home, and retirement. There are others. The adjustment to the loss is a process. I have given a large amount of space to what grief is and what it does because being sensitive to the grievers and learning to pray for them requires an understanding of what is happening in their lives.

Who the Grievers Are

There is no way a person can be unaffected by loss. In one way or another, every choice a person makes involves some loss. With many of the choices we make, we know in advance what some of the emotional fallout will be, but the knowing doesn't keep the fallout from occurring. A young adult leaving his parents' home to be on his own feels the emotional tug as he makes his plans to leave. Even when a choice like this is anticipated and planned, it still causes a crisis, a change in the normal routine. Other crises occur over which we have no control. These crises make us aware that life is no longer as it once was. That is a loss. The following prayer expresses some of the emotions and struggles any crisis may precipitate.

Father,

I feel like I have lived a lifetime in the last seven days. Crisis events are like that. They cause a gamut of feelings, better described as an emotional roller coaster. One moment I was in the valley of despair. The next moment, I was climbing the peak of exhilaration, only suddenly to feel like I was being flung over the brink into emptiness. Seemingly, the least significant event became paramount. I wanted to examine every detail. A word like *mainly* spoken in conversation required interpretation.

Much of my life has been up for review. It may have been the most intense week of my life. I have a very different view of life this Monday than last. Last Monday I felt nothing. Today I am on a mountain, looking out at the terrain and seeing a road marked

"Hope" which I shall travel. Last week only intellectually was I confident of your presence. In reflection, I realize I felt an undergirding. That was you, wasn't it, Lord? Today, I sense you out ahead, pulling me toward you. I am eager to be drawn by you. I know the journey will have both sorrow and joy. I am willing to risk the sorrow to experience the joy. In some way the two are related. A college student said it best, "If there is no pain in the good-bye, there can be no joy in the hello."

I guess we constantly are saying good-bye to one part of life and hello to another. Graduations, marriages, births, and deaths are mixtures of good-byes and hellos. Marriage and family conflict call for saying good-bye to situations as they used to be or we dreamed they would be and hello to the way things are. There is pain. There is joy. Thank you for being God of my pain and God of my joy in the lifetime I have lived this week. Amen.

You probably can identify with some portion of this prayer. That is evidence that all of us are the grievers. Now I want to write about some specific grievers and share prayers that I have written for them to illustrate learning to pray for the grief sufferers.

The Marrying. Who would think there would be any grief related to a wedding? Anyone who has ever married will tell you that there is. Any parent who has had a child who married also will tell you there is grief at a wedding. Some of the grief is the result of conflict and strife the family had buried, but the tension came rising to the surface under the pressure of the marriage crisis. Parents come to celebrate the marriage feast of their children and discover emotions welling up inside and sometimes spilling over their cheeks as tears. These often are identified as tears of joy. Maybe they are, but they also reveal the pain of change and loss. The parents' feelings are saying, "He/she will always be my child but the relationship will be different now. He/she has been dependent on me but now the relationship will be one of interdependency at best and independency at worst."

The siblings of those being married may be overcome with emotion, usually sadness. They see life changing almost before their eyes. This one who has been a part of life won't be present anymore. That leaves an empty chair at the table, but more significantly, an empty place in life. Joy for the one marrying diminishes neither the pain of the loss nor the emptiness felt.

Jokes are made about the groom or bride being nervous. I have yet to meet an unnervous bride or groom. Why should the couple not be uneasy? They are venturing into a relationship and commitment in which they have no way of knowing what will happen. One man, after nearly forty years of marriage, said that on his wedding day he had no idea that the "better" could be so good and the "worse" could be so bad. The bride and groom, regardless of how well they know each other, are leaving the familiar surroundings of family relationships they have known for twenty years or more. They are venturing into a relationship with someone each has known for two or three years, and most of the time it has been as "Mr. and Ms Nice Fiance."

In 1969 I stood in the front of a sanctuary and looked down the aisle at a beautiful bride. In fifteen minutes I would be married to her. For two years we had talked, planned, and anticipated this day. It was what we both wanted. Then I felt a flood of fear pour over me. I felt my face blend in with my white shirt, my legs felt like water. I was scared, and I was scared that I was scared. What was happening to me? I was taking an irreversible action. No longer was marriage a dream or conversation. It was soon to be a reality. Life would be different from that point, but exactly how life would be was unknown. I was leaving singleness, leaving my parents and my sister. I knew I could not go back home.

Those who marry have some of these feelings, as well as many other hopes and fears. Learning to pray for those who are marrying involves empathy—putting ourselves in their places—the places of the bride and groom and of course the parents, siblings, and friends—and then communicating to God our concerns and desires for all those who are grieving. Perhaps it can be seen more clearly at marriage than anywhere that grief involves saying good-bye to some aspects of life and hello to others. Here is a prayer for a couple in which I expressed my care for them.

Thank you, Father, that John and Susan invited us to celebrate with them the most important day in their lives. Their nervousness and ours indicates something of the significance and seriousness of marriage.

Thank you, Lord, for the gift of life in the beautiful packages of John and Susan. Thank you that their parents sought to nurture and guide John and Susan out of dependence upon them and into dependence upon you.

Their parents are delighted for John and Susan, and yet there is some pain. It is hard for them to imagine that these they held in their arms are now ready to hold each other. It seems only yesterday that John and Susan were running to mom and dad to show them the gap where a tooth was or crying out for the comfort of a parent's lap because of a scraped knee. It doesn't seem that long ago that John didn't notice girls and Susan didn't notice boys. Now, their eyes sparkle when they look at each other. Support their parents as they say good-bye to the son or daughter they once knew and hello to the man or woman they are becoming.

Father, John and Susan's brothers and sisters are glad and sad today. They are glad for John and Susan because they want to give themselves in marriage to each other. Their brothers and sisters are sad for themselves. Right now they feel like they are losing a part of themselves, and that is an empty feeling.

We have heard it said that at marriage a man and woman are to leave their families and give themselves to each other. John and Susan want to do that, Lord, but they cannot without some pain and struggle. They are saying good-bye to a life they have known and hello to a life together that is unknown. They are excited and frightened. Calm their fears, Lord, with your presence and guidance. As they commit themselves to each other, may they promise not only to allow but also to help each other to grow. May they be encouragers to one another. May their love for you and for each other deepen each day and burn away the impurities in their lives. May their youthful fascination grow toward mature charm. As time and trials leave traces upon their faces, may they keep holding hands in the dark, keep reaching for each other, and keep tuning their love.

Now, Father, may your love that will not let us go enrich John and Susan and give them hope and help today and every day for as long as they live. Amen.

The Life Givers. Would you think any grief would be felt or expressed when a child is born? The argument goes that childbirth is such a happy occasion, why would anyone be sad? Of course, if the child is born with some handicap or abnormality we readily understand the disappointment and the hurt. What about the couple or the single mother who is planning for the birth of a child? Is there good-bye and hello in the process? I think there is. The couple expecting their first child experiences some grief. There are those who say to them, "That baby is going to change your lives," as if the child were a plague of some sort. There will be change because, until the birth of the child, there were just the two of them. They have had flexibility in their schedule. Flexibility can continue after the arrival of a child, but the intensity level increases because another person's needs must be considered in decisions like going out for pizza, taking a weekend trip, or doing the grocery shopping. The chance for a couple to converse uninterrupted ends with the arrival of a child. The communication lines triple with the birth of the first child and double again with the second child, and now they have increased sixfold from the time when there were no children.

More physical and psychic space are needed. Health concerns increase, as do nights of interrupted rest. Parenting is a joyful part of life for many, but the choice to have children is a choice that results in loss. Once again there is good-bye and hello.

Eternal lover of children, thank you that Jim and Joan could be partners with you in the lifegiving process. They are delighted that Susie is a healthy, full-term infant. They are eager to be the kind of parents Susie needs.

Father, Jim and Joan have some ambivalent feelings about this new, unknown stage of life. Although they decided together to be parents and have spent the last nine months preparing for Susie's arrival, they have some feelings that trouble them. Already they miss those quiet evenings by the fire when it was just the two of them. They are fearful that Susie will come between them. Help them, Father, to love Susie but not to dote on her. Help Jim and Joan to continue to find time for each other. That won't be as easy now, but don't let them give up. May they see that the best way for Susie to feel secure and loved is for them to continue nurturing their love for each other.

Sometimes they may wish they didn't have Susie. Let them know you understand. When they recall the "good old days," help them to season those memories with a large dose of reality and to go light on the nostalgia.

Father, now Jim and Joan will be parents for as long as they live, and they will be spouses that long too. May they be honest with their feelings of loss as they journey through the change so they may in the proper way and at the proper time say good-bye to the newlywed phase of their lives and hello to the parenting phase. I offer this prayer in the manner in which I think Jesus would pray. Amen.

The Graduates. In August 1965, I packed my bags, put them in the family car, and with my parents, sister, uncle, and aunt, made the two and one-half hours' drive from Monticello to Georgetown, Kentucky. My college education was beginning. Life would never be the same for me in Monticello again, although I did not know that at the time. I was excited to be at college. As I said good-bye to my family, it happened. Mother had controlled herself as long as she could. The tears began to flow. I was surprised at her response. I had not sensed the impact that this event represented for my family and for me. I was leaving home.

The word *commencement* had been confusing to me for a long time. Why did an educational process end with a ceremony that was called "beginning"? Now I began to understand. The end of one phase of life is the beginning of another.

When a person graduates from high school, college, graduate or professional school, she has a sense of fulfillment and fear. She has achieved an objective toward which she has worked and her diploma says she is qualified. For what? There is the fear. What if she cannot measure up to the expectations? What about those parents who don't want to let go? Should she stay with them or go off on her own? How can she negotiate this passage in life? The following prayer expresses some of my concerns for one graduate.

> Lord, I can tell by looking at Diane that she is sitting on top of the world. Why shouldn't she feel good about herself? Let her bask in the warmth of accomplishment for awhile.
>
> Lord, I think Diane knows she can't enjoy the euphoria forever. Already she feels the sadness of saying good-bye to friends. She knows that probably all of them will never be back together again. She struggles with the question of what to do, who to be. People have been asking for years what she wants to be. Lord, she wants to be an adult. Help her to become one.
>
> Already Diane is being bombarded with decisions to make. College? Professional school? Vocation? Moratorium? What should she do, Father? Help her find her way. Be a compass for her to aid her in finding direction.
>
> Diane struggles with leaving home, Father. She really would like to be out on her own, but what if she fails? What if she can't make it out there in the world that looms so large on the horizon?
>
> Assure her that you are with her. She probably will fail at some things. Be with her in her failures and help her to learn from them. Protect her from the trap of the world's success which is defined by power and greed. Help her to love people and use things rather than to love things and use people. May life for Diane be a continual unfolding of her gifts and abilities. May she be aware of your desire to help her to be a person of love, sensitivity, and understanding. May her encounter of this unknown prepare her for the facing of the many additional unknowns that will be part of her life. Amen.

Graduation highlights what is true every day in a less intense way. People do not begin a new day where the previous day ended. Because of our choices and decisions, as well as the actions of others, all of us, but especially graduates, are sojourners and pilgrims in strange and foreign lands. At some point the graduates need to sit down and weep before they can move on to make music with their lives.

The Empty Nesters. The emotional surprise that overtakes many parents at the graduation of a child is just the beginning of the adjustment process identified as "the empty nest." Some parents feel the first twinges of this experience when their youngest child begins school. For others the emotional pulls are felt at some event in the life of a child that says to mom and dad that he's growing up and growing away from them. Although a major parenting task is to relate to and interact with a child so that he can become his own person separate from his parents, the separating is not without sadness and struggle.

The separating of children from their parents occurs a little at a time. Parents may first notice it when a child discovers a friend in the neighborhood with whom he likes to play at age two and one-half or three years. The child's world is expanding and now there are influences other than mom, dad, and siblings. However, the jolt of this separating is felt when the last child leaves home. Now, husband and wife are back where they started, just the two of them, but they can never go back to where they started. They have invested themselves in those who have left. A part of themselves is gone. The physical and emotional letting go do not happen simultaneously. Long after the kids are gone, mom and dad are still missing them. The "nest" is empty and it takes some grieving to adjust. The following prayer expresses some of my concerns for one couple who were "empty nesters."

Lord,
Bob and Carol are struggling. They don't seem to have any motivation. Sometimes they don't seem to know what to do with themselves. There's nothing on television. They barely scan the newspaper. When they go out to eat, they just dawdle over their food, like the kids used to do. That's where the pain is, isn't it, Lord?

The kids are grown and gone. That's what Bob and Carol wanted to happen, but it hurts. I saw it in their eyes when I mentioned Susan's name. Then they put it into words. For years their house was too small, now it's too big. How many meals did they eat complaining about the noise and wishing for some peace and quiet? They have the quiet now, but they don't sense any peace. Their house hasn't been this quiet for twenty-five years.

Lord, this is a difficult time of transition for Bob and Carol. They get on each other's nerves. Now that they have uninterrupted time for each other, they seem only to want to talk about the kids being gone and that hurts so much that they don't talk about it. God, help them to talk about their pain and to discover through their painful dialogue that they have more to talk about than their children. Guide them to talk about each other and help them to renew the romance of their marriage. Bob and Carol both feel the pain of their loss. May their pain be an entrance to a relationship of deeper commitment to each other rather than an exit leading to a broken relationship. Amen.

The Divorcing. I have never met a person who was divorcing who was not hurting. Even those who years earlier divorced emotionally but remained legally married for the children's sake, or for a number of other reasons, hurt at the time the divorce is finalized. Both those who make every effort to get their marriage to work and those who seem to make no effort experience pain when divorce occurs. Many factors contribute to the pain. Marriage may not be what the couple had hoped. They have been unable to accomplish what they intended, and so they feel a sense of failure. Each feels wronged in the relationship, and each has contributed to the failure of the relationship. In spite of the relief of tension the divorce brings, there also is the fear of what life will be like as a divorcee.

Often the church adds salt to the burning wounds of those divorcing. The church more easily practices rejection rather than redemption with regard to those divorcing. The one place that persons in need ought to be able to turn is the church. While the church must work toward strengthening relationships and improving family life, it must also minister to those whose most intimate relationships have disintegrated.

One of the most significant things I can do for the divorcing is to pray for them. For me to pray for the divorcing is not an arm's length distancing me from them; rather, to pray for them means I am embracing them, taking their pain and hurt as my own and communicating with God about the agony that is felt.

Father, after fourteen years of marriage, Pat and Sue are calling it quits. They're cashing in their marriage chips today. When and where did they go wrong? Sue said it began years ago when she started to feel intimidated by Pat. Since he hit her, she has been frightened to disagree with him. Pat says the problems began when Sue went to work two years ago. All those women at work convinced Sue how great single life is, according to Pat.

This marriage has been in trouble a long time, and so much damage has been done that neither Pat nor Sue is willing to risk the hurt to invest in rebuilding the relationship. Father, comfort them in their hurt and their lost dreams. Each of them hurts and at times wants to hurt the other in return. I see this most clearly in their arguments about custody of the children.

The children already feel in the middle. They are convinced that somehow they are responsible for this divorce. Help the children to know that isn't true. Lord, protect Pat and Sue from damaging each other and their children any more than already has occurred.

Sometimes, Lord, I think they are deciding who wins and who loses by who gets the children. Help them to see that there are no winners in divorce. Help Pat and Sue to keep from counting the ways they have been hurt or searching for ways to hurt in return. Every month when he sends the child-support payment and she receives it, they will remember what used to be and never can be again. When the children make plans to visit him, Pat and Sue will remember. When decisions concerning the children have to be made, they will remember.

Father, help Sue and Pat to admit their marriage has ended. Protect them from holding on to false hopes of reconciliation. Protect their self-esteem from erosion by guilt and self-pity. Enable them to admit their wrongs to you. Cleanse them and make them whole. Guide them in redirecting and rebuilding their lives. Help them to be whole persons, wholly committed to you. Amen.

The Midlifer. Midlife crisis is a phenomenon that has been identified in recent years. Some say it is a luxury problem of an affluent culture. Others suggest that only now are people examining more carefully the developmental stages of adulthood as the stages of infancy, childhood, and adolescence have been examined in the past. Whatever explanation is given for midlife crisis, many people come to a time, generally between the ages of thirty-five and fifty, where their lives seem to be up for review. Several factors contribute to this crisis which alters, if not halts, one's normal routine by causing one to examine why one is doing what one is doing.

Near thirty-five or beyond, a person begins realizing that his life is half over. If he has accomplished everything he intended, then he has no horizons toward which to look. The usual case, however, is that the midlifer is aware that he hasn't achieved all he desired, and being realistic he sees that some of his dreams will go unfulfilled. Now some things that had been low in his priority list begin to take on increasing significance.

This season of life is a rocky period of transition. It often occurs at or near the time the children are grown and leaving home and at a time when vocationally a person seems to be at the peak of one's professional productivity. For some it is catch-up time emotionally. Human beings develop through stages. To skip or avoid a stage cannot last forever. Eventually the person reverts to that stage and catches up on that part of one's development. Midlife seems to be one of the catch-up phases for adults. The following prayer expresses some of my concerns for one of the midlifers I have known.

Lord,

It's been a six-month roller coaster ride for Mike. Change is never easy, but mid-life career change seems to create stress like nothing else. For twenty-seven years Mike worked for the same employer. Why did he get out? There are many factors, but one strong one was the clear message that he didn't fit in with the current program. That hurts. I get angry for him and with him.

I'm glad he has retirement income, but that doesn't compensate for over-the-shoulder looking, second-guessing, and what-am-I-going-to-do-with-the-rest-of-my-life feelings. His life has been so structured for years, and now it is almost totally unstructured. Some mornings he feels very brave, but by noon he wishes he weren't so brave. Other mornings he just feels numb and by noon he is down on every decision he has ever made. He wants a job, but not just any job. He left just any job, which is what it had become, because he was not using his skills. His next job needs to be fulfilling and to have purpose. This raises the question of worth. Mike raises it. No one else does. Friends reveal their insensitivity when they ask, "Are you working?" "Did you get a job yet?"

Jo Ann doesn't know what to do. She's not used to Mike being home for dinner on time. It's nice having him around, and sometimes it's not so nice. Jo Ann is adjusting too.

Mike and Jo Ann seem to have an abundance of energy. They are looking for worthwhile investments. Help them, Father, to find constructive channels for their energy and gifts so they will be good stewards of their time, energy, and gifts. May they find worth together in being rather than in doing, so that your grace may permeate their lives. Amen.

The Mover. We are people on the move. So what else is new? The early Hebrews were nomadic people, pitching their tents here and there. One of many distinctions between them and us is that, when they pulled up stakes the whole community, the whole tribe pulled up stakes, while for us only the nuclear family moves from one community to another. This individual movement, coupled with the societal mobility in the latter half of the twentieth century, has increased and compounded the grief experiences for people in our society.

One personal example will illustrate the mobility change from one generation to another. I lived in and grew up in the same house from birth until I went to college. My parents have since moved twice, but both times within the same small community. My oldest child moved twice before she was six years old. Each of these moves were over six hundred miles. Who knows how many more moves she will make in her lifetime, involving good-byes and hellos? Prior to her last move, she learned a verse that helped sustain her during the transition.

> Make new friends but keep the old;
> One is silver and the other gold.

There are moves in addition to the geographical ones involving events, such as vocational change and retirement. There are times when these types of moves do not result in geographical uprooting, but they are painful, nevertheless, as change occurs. This is experienced in organizations through promotions, resignations, or retirements and the person remains involved with many to whom one related previously. One example is a church staff member who resigned his position because of health problems and remained an active participant in the congregation. Here is a prayer I offered for him and for us.

Father,

April 6, 1969, was a very good day. That was when Leonard Lane became assistant to the pastor. *Supportive* is a word that describes Leonard. He is an encourager, a modern-day Barnabas ("son of encouragement").

During these thirteen years Leonard has been a present help in time of trouble. Father, I am grateful for the help and hope you have given to others through Leonard. Thank you for the support and encouragement you have offered me through him.

April 30 is a very sad day. This is the day when Leonard ends his role as assistant to the pastor. This is a sad day for Leonard because it is not what he wants to do; rather, it is what he has to do for his health's sake. It really is Leonard's integrity that precipitated this decision. He could have been a hanger-on, but he could not live with himself if he were not able to give his all to the task. Leonard has been able to give of himself to others through this position. I know he will continue to give of himself but the change causes its own sadness.

We feel the loss too—our loss. We are comforted knowing Leonard will remain a participant in this congregation. It is easier for us to say good-bye to the position than to say good-bye to the person.

Now, Father, as Leonard leaves one phase of service and seeks to take up another, may the road rise to meet him, may the wind be always at his back, and may you continue to hold him in the palm of your hand. Amen.

The Aging. Many of us realize that physically we are unable to do what we used to do. We may not be as quick in a game or able to finish a task as rapidly now. These changes are difficult for us to admit at first. As we discover, however, that we do some things better now because of experience, confidence, and competence, we feel our lives are in better balance. With nearly every passing year, we become more conscious of death; but we are not as willing to admit to aging, except as we see it in others.

Aging is one of those processes that does not seem to apply to us. The older we become, the more we increase our chances of encountering diseases and accidents that can disable us. I have discovered for myself that I do not fear death nearly so much as I fear debilitating illness or accident that would disable me and force me to be dependent physically upon my wife or children or friends.

The aging process often causes a person to say good-bye to first one phase of life and then another and another. This results in compounded grief, and often the griever feels that life is collapsing on every hand. Dreams and plans are interrupted, halted; some of them never to be. These unfulfilled dreams perhaps are as prevalent near retirement as any time. Many people plan for and anticipate retirement for years, but then must shift, alter, and, in some cases, radically change all of those plans because of accident, disease, or death of a companion. The following prayer expresses my concern for a couple whose retirement plans were altered radically because of disease.

Lord,
    Emajean and Bob need your help and hope.
    They had exciting plans for retirement. Trips to take, stamps and coins to organize, flowers and vegetables to raise. Now they can't do any of these.
    Bob has struggled with Parkinson's disease for ten years. Then the hyperglycemia developed. Now Bob's mind does not function as it once did.
    He was such a bright person, a small, caring, quiet, organized man who got the job done.
    Now he can follow only one brief instruction at a time, if that.
    At times Emajean cannot bear to admit what she is seeing and

feeling. Now she has retired to take care of Bob. This wasn't what she had planned for retirement. Her patience runs out by noon every day. Forty years ago when she said, "For better or for worse, in sickness and in health," she did not know that "worse" and "sickness" meant this.

Will Bob's illness consume Emajean as it has consumed him? O God, Emajean needs your help. Sustain and strengthen her today.

What hope is there for Bob and Emajean? Quality of life for Bob has degenerated rapidly in the last four years. At times he is only a trembling shell. What hope does Emajean have? She can reminisce about how things used to be. That results in anger. She can recall the support Bob was to her during the years she battled cancer. That obligates her. She can anticipate Bob's death. That saddens her. She can plan what she will do after Bob dies. That makes her feel guilty. She can bring all these things to you, and she does.

Emajean has trouble on every hand, but she knows she is not without friends. She is working at living one day at a time, and it is work. It is difficult for her not to worry about tomorrow, but she is learning that she cannot face tomorrow without the resources of today.

She needs your help to live all of today before she tries to live tomorrow.

There is hope for Emajean and it rests in you.

Thank you, Father. Amen.

The Dying. If we live very long, we will have opportunity to visit with someone who is dying. Medical progress has increased life expectancy and life support systems sustain for longer periods of time those who are dying. Although the opportunity to be with the dying is available, many choose to avoid the dying because of their fear of death. Although persons who are dying generally want to talk about what is happening to them with those who are important to them, often those closest to them find conversation about dying to be very difficult.

I want my life to have meaning for as long as I am alive. I have sensed this to be the desire of those who were dying whom I have known.

Every one of them wanted to get well; but when it had been determined that would not happen, then each wanted to make the most of the remainder of his or her life. It is a narrow place to journey between the desire to live and the inevitability of death. Terminally ill persons are more conscious of this narrow corridor than the rest of us who also are living with only a heartbeat separating us from life and death. The meaning of life often is highlighted for the dying as they find a reason for living and set their sights on it. It may be a family reunion or a child's wedding or graduation. There are those for whom life will end soon who seem to keep on planning and hoping, not as a means of denying what is occurring in their lives, but as a way of saying, "My life isn't over until it's over." One example illustrates this.

My uncle, for whom I was named, was a truck driver all his adult life. He owned a pickup truck for his personal use. Cancer was diagnosed in November. Surgery was scheduled for December, delayed until January, and then canceled because the malignancy was a rapidly progressing type and surgery would be of no benefit. In February this man bought a new pickup truck. Some would say, "What a waste." But for him it was a symbol of hope. This action was similar to that of Jeremiah (32:6ff.), who invested in real estate when it appeared that all Israel would be destroyed. Jeremiah's hope was in God, symbolized in his land purchase. The truck driver's hope was in God, symbolized for him in a new pickup truck sitting in the driveway. God had been with him on all his other journeys. He had every reason to believe God would be with him on this last journey.

Being with the dying has sensitized me to their needs. Usually their needs are not what one expects. Often we anticipate that the dying would want to get well or want to avoid any conversation about death. That may be our agenda, not theirs. What they want is strength and courage for the living of the days they have. They want to be as comfortable as possible, and they do not want to be a burden to anyone. When life can no longer be lived with dignity and meaning, they want to die. Being able to pray for the dying with these things in mind is helpful for the dying, their family and friends, and for me.

Recently I visited a man in the hospital whom I had known for five years. He had been battling cancer for seven years and had had several remissions. The day of this visit, he was very weak, breathing was difficult, and he had been unable to eat solid foods for several days. His appearance told me he probably would not live more than another day. I was not certain that he was conscious, but when I spoke, he replied. I visited in the room with his wife and daughters for several minutes. Before leaving, I asked him if he wanted me to have a prayer, and he said, "Yes." As I held his hand, this is the prayer I offered for him. I don't know who was strengthened the most through our communion with God—the man, his wife, his daughters, or me.

Father,
    You have been a constant source of strength to Everett through this journey, and we are very grateful for that. There is a sense in which this is the most difficult day of Everett's life, a day of saying good-bye to his family. There are three things that he needs today, Father. He needs help, hope, and strength. All of these things you can give him. Give them to him today, Father. Amen.

As I said, "Amen," Everett firmly gripped my hand as if to shake hands and said, "Amen," which means, "So be it." Everett died later that evening.

The Bereaved. I have indicated throughout this chapter that all of us are grievers because of loss. Certainly the most shattering form of grief is caused by the death of a significant person in an individual's life. These grievers I identify as the bereaved. Generally, the longer and more intimate the relationship, the more deeply the bereaved person feels the loss of the one who has died.

I have seen my father cry twice. The first time was when his father died, and the second time was when he told me about the death of his army buddy who probably was the closest friend he ever had and very near to his age. The age factor often personalizes death and bereavement more than any single factor. Here is a prayer I prayed for someone whose friend was dying. The two were close emotionally and chronologically.

O God,
    George is so distraught today. He called from another city

because the grief is so heavy. I ache with him as he sighs and moans for Carl. Carl can't live long. Maybe a month or two. Cancer in the bone marrow. They've been friends for years. There's only two years' difference in their ages. They started a church together. They know what kinds of bricks and mortar it takes to make a church building. They have been members of each other's church for thirty years. George dies a little every day, God, because Carl dies a little every day. It just isn't fair! George is helpless. I feel helpless. It's a dead end.

God, there have been a few times in George's life when he flew like an eagle. When his boys were born. When his grandson was born. When the congregation moved into the sanctuary. A lot of times George has been able to run and not get tired. When he finished college. Cheering the boys on at swim meets. Reflecting on life with Suzanne. But God, it is all George can do today to walk and not faint. And he can do that because he is leaning on you.

O Father, George needs your support. Hold him up. Help him to grieve with hope. Amen.

Death causes the bereaved to recall qualities which the deceased had that those grieving appreciate and would like to emulate. The following prayer expresses appreciation to God for some of the characteristics friends expressed about someone who died whom I did not know well.

Lord,

I met him at church a couple of times. Church isn't a bad place to meet people. I only knew John through his family and friends. I'm thankful to you for the gift of life shared with us through John's life.

John was a conscientious friend. I don't know what it would be like to be friendless. I do know that it was not possible to be friendless if John were around. Apparently, he lived the philosophy that the best way to have friends is to be a friend. John knew that the grass is always greener where you water it. He was a friend to several people for more than three decades. That is staying power. I am grateful, Father, for John's conscientious friendship.

I am reminded of your staying power, Lord. There are many enemies, but we are never without a friend. Your promise never to leave me or forget me sustains me today as I say good-bye to John. You are my Friend, my constant Companion. You can be trusted. Thank you for modeling friendship in John. Amen.

I am a minister. My profession puts me in contact with people who are dying and with their families and friends who are bereaved. As a pastor I develop relationships with members of the congregation. I am not unaffected by what happens to them. Betty was a parishioner who struggled with cancer for two years. She was open with me about her living and her dying. Her death evoked the following prayer from me.

Lord,

I've tried, but I can't remember when I first met Betty. I remember hearing her read to young children. I can see her in her pew. I can feel her warm greeting after worship service.

I can remember our conversation over strawberry pie at a Labor Day picnic. There was nothing gregarious about her in those encounters. Rather, they revealed a mild-mannered, soft-spoken, courageous woman. That was Betty.

God, I still recall my visit with Betty on Wednesday. I said, "Well, it looks like time is running out for you." And she said, with affirmation and without a tear, "Yes, it is, and I am ready to die." I melted inside, and I felt my eyes fill with tears as I wondered if that might be my last conversation with her—and it was.

Lord, Betty wanted quality of life and quantity of days. When it became evident that she could not have both, she chose quality of life. I hope I can do that. Lord, help me to do that now.

Betty is dead now. I'm realizing it a little at a time. I don't know what lies beyond death, but Father, I know that you are on both sides of death.

Give me the courage to face this hour. Grant me the strength to live this day. Amen.

I have identified some of the grief-causing experiences common through the ages and stages of life. No doubt you can think of others. Grief is our response to loss, and none of us are exempt. The grief process is an occasion for us to commune with God and to continue learning to pray for the grief sufferers. Perhaps when we pray for the grievers, more than at any other time, we are praying for ourselves.

Notes

1. From a lecture given by Ned Cassem, psychiatrist, Harvard University, April 1979, at Johns Hopkins Hospital.

2. Granger Westberg, *Good Grief* (Philadelphia: Fortress Press, 1962).

6

Learning to Pray for Public Worship

O give thanks to the Lord, for he is good;
   for his steadfast love endures for ever!
Let the redeemed of the Lord say so,
   who he has redeemed from trouble
and gathered in from the lands,
   from the east and from the west,
from the north and from the south.
Whoever is wise, let him give heed to these things;
   let me consider the steadfast love of the Lord (Ps. 107:1-3,43).

George Buttrick, a great Presbyterian pulpiteer, said that for every minute he spent in the pulpit, he spent an hour in preparation. A significant part of his preparation involved the prayers to be offered in public worship. He said, "If you must choose between getting the sermon right and getting the prayers right, get the prayers right!"[1]

Much of the learning about how to pray occurs in public worship. Perhaps this explains partially why prayer often is meaningless and we feel we do not know how to pray. Is it not logical for a person who is wondering about how to pray to decide that the way prayers are prayed in public worship must be how one is to pray?

The natural setting for public prayer is public worship. I need to express some things about public worship before I discuss learning to pray for public worship. Then I will identify a variety of kinds of prayers used in public worship.

Public Worship

Worship is natural behavior for us because we are creatures with the ability of self-consciousness. We can ascribe value and worth to something outside ourselves which we consider to be of ultimate significance. Worship can refer to the reverence we hold for any object of ultimate worth. The Christian concept of God is that he is personal; therefore, public worship is communion of persons with the Person.

Worship is an event, an encounter between the living Lord and his people. Worship is not "going to church." It is taking our places in the congregation and contributing ourselves in appreciation to God and communion with him. Christian worship is our attempt to express appreciation to God our Creator, to offer ourselves as living sacrifices to God our Redeemer, and to have communion with God our Sustainer. Christian worship is the conscious awareness of the living God and a conscious attempt to respond to the loving activity of God with a living, vibrant faith.

The public worship of God has come under much criticism in recent years, perhaps in all years. It is not uncommon to hear someone say of public worship, "There is nothing in it for me." This probably says more about the speaker than it says about worship, although enough public worship has been sloppily and slovenly done to give a person data to support such a statement. Public worship that is done with preparation and purpose might cause a person to say, "There is nothing in me for it, but I must remedy this deficiency."

Public Prayer

Since worship is the only thing we can do to God, the entire public worship event is a type of prayer to God. Communion with God involves communication, and prayer is the vehicle of our communication with God.

Much of the praying that occurs in public worship is public prayer because the prayers are overheard by others. James Martineau suggested our need for public prayers when he said that the tender voices of the Spirit are easily lost; therefore, we need to overhear each other.

Public prayer often enables people to center their thoughts because there is a leveling of life through prayer. For many worshipers, the public prayers of worship aid in calming their restlessness. Augustine's truth surfaces, "We are restless until we rest in Thee." Public prayer does not accost God with what we want, nor should it be used to flatter God.

Rather, public prayer assists us in attaching our minds and hearts to the One with whom we are eager to relate.

Prayer offered in public, whether spoken antiphonally, in unison, or with one person verbalizing for all, thaws one's personal loyalties and indifference and puts one in community. William Fox sees public prayer as both observation and revelation. As observation, it serves as both a microscope and a telescope. Public prayer as a microscope helps us see and admit that we are not perfect. As a telescope, public prayer causes us to see many needs and to discover that our needs and struggles are universal. Public prayer also is revelation. It is a time when we express to God something of who we are as a corporate body. The more we reveal of ourselves, the more receptive we seem to become to God's disclosure of himself to us.

More than any other aspect of public worship, public prayer helps us understand genuine worship. Often we have considered worship as a drama in which God is the prompter, the worship leaders are the actors, and the congregation is the audience. Authentic prayer is directed to God and there is the cue for us. Danish theologian Soren Kierkegaard appropriately described worship as a drama where the congregation are the actors, the worship leaders are the prompters, and God is the audience. Worship is the only thing we can do to God.

While conversing with Jack Averill, he commented that he viewed public prayer as rehearsal. That was an intriguing observation that at first suggested to me that public prayer was not real prayer; however, any serious rehearsal is hard work in preparation of the actual event. *Rehearsal* is of French derivation and means to harrow again, originally in the sense of breaking up and leveling plowed ground. Public prayer is rehearsal in that it churns up, disturbs, and makes one uncomfortable, so that in private prayer the individual will commune with God about personal issues that he needs God's help in resolving.

This understanding of public prayer calls for serious preparation of public prayers. For some the preparation will include writing out the prayers for public worship, while for others preparation involves thinking through what one will address to God in prayer. Every effort needs to be made to compose and shape worship prayers that are true to the ways of God and faithful to the needs of people. Of course, Puritanism continues to have its influence on us. There are those who stringently oppose prepared or written prayers. Their argument often is that to prepare prayers is to squelch the Spirit; however, if the Holy Spirit can inspire one to pray spontaneously, then the same Holy Spirit ought to be able to inspire one to prepare a prayer. To review routinely one's written prayers is a helpful corrective to vain repetition and empty phrases. Often as preparation for prayer is made, it is discovered that the prayer prepares the person.

Many are serious in their desire to learn to pray. The best opportunity for instruction is through the prayers of public worship. Here is where modeling of prayer occurs for the individual; thus, public prayer is rehearsal for private prayer. Perhaps this is why Buttrick insisted that we get the prayers right.

Prayers for Public Worship

As I prepare prayers for public worship, I attempt to envision the needs of the congregation. In my mind, I walk the aisles of the sanctuary visualizing members of the congregation, recalling what their faces say to me, as well as remembering their joys and their sorrows, the accomplishments and struggles that are theirs. Then I consider how these concerns may be common to all of us and how they can be expressed to God through prayer while respecting the anonymity of congregants.

Part of my preparation for prayer includes consideration of community, national, and world events that impact on congregants' lives. How to formulate concerns about these events is part of learning to pray for public worship.

A variety of types and styles of prayers may be used in public worship. Prayer in public worship serves a priestly function because it is the vehicle for presenting the people's situations to God.

Call to Worship

The intent of the call to worship is to summon worshipers to unite in corporate worship. The call to worship is a prayer in the sense that worshipers are invited to dedicate themselves to God through worship. The words of the call to worship may be spoken or sung. If spoken, they may be spoken by one person, expressed in unison by the congregation, or read responsively. Passages of Scripture, especially some of the psalms, may be adapted as calls to worship. A variety of calls to worship follow as illustrations.

Responsive Calls to Worship

(1) Leader: Praise the Lord, my soul,
     Congregation: And do not forget how kind he is.
     Leader: He forgives all my sins.
     Congregation: And heals all my diseases.
     Leader: He keeps me from the grave.
     Congregation: And blesses me with love and mercy.
     Leader: He does not punish us as we deserve.
     Congregation: Or repay us for our sins and wrongs.
     Leader: As far as the east is from the west,
     Congregation: So far does he remove our sins from us.
     Leader: As kind as a parent is to his children,
     Congregation: So kind is the Lord to those who honor him.
     Leader: He knows what we are made of;
     Congregation: He remembers that we are dust.
     Leader: For those who honor the Lord, his love lasts forever,
     Congregation: And his goodness endures for all generations.
     Leader: The Lord placed his throne in heaven;
     Congregation: He is king over all.
     Leader: Praise the Lord,
     Congregation: All his creatures in all the places he rules.
     All: Praise the Lord, my soul!

Adapted from Psalm 103

(2) Leader: Welcome to the house of the people of the Lord. Why
             are you here?
     Congregation: We are here to worship God; to see visions
                    with the foresight of youth, to dream
                    dreams with the wisdom of age, to move
                    mountains with the power of faith.
     Leader: We are a daring people;
     Congregation: Daring to believe that what happens in this

hour matters to God, daring to believe that
what happens in this hour will be
life-changing for us.

Leader: Welcome to the house of the people of the Lord.

Unison Calls to Worship

(1)   I was glad when they said to me, "Let us go into the house
of the Lord." And now we are here. Let us pray for the peace of
our city. May there be peace inside these walls and safety in our
houses. For the sake of our relatives and friends may peace abide.
For the glory of God may peace abide. May our worship of God
today transform us into makers of peace. I am glad they said to
me, "Let us go into the house of the Lord."

Adapted from Psalm 122

(2)   Father,

We are aware of our great dependence upon you. We think
only briefly before we realize how finite we are and how infinite
you are. We plan only shortly before we discover that you are the
Master Designer of the universe. We give thought to ourselves
only briefly before we realize with awe-filled beings that you care
for us, that you have given us life, and that you are inviting us to
relate to you. How, O Father, might we relate to you? What might
we do to you, our Creator? Worship you? We are awed because
we matter to you. It is true that all we could ever do to you and for
you is to worship you, isn't it?

Lord, may that be what happens in us in this place, in this hour.
Amen.

Individual Calls to Worship

(1)   We come together to worship God as eagerly as Jesus of
Nazareth strode toward the Jordan River. The faith of our Lord
plunged him into the water. May our faith immerse us in worship
and enable us to wade into the deep waters of life with confidence
and hope. May our journey through this worship service model for
us our journey of living this week. We come to worship God
eagerly and faithfully.

(2) Lift up your eyes and see the work of God in fellow worshipers and in yourself.

Lift up your ears and hear the word of God recorded in Scripture, alive in each other.

Lift up your minds and think the thoughts of God after him and with him.

Lift up your hearts and feel the presence of God in our midst.

Lift up your lives and worship the Lord your God with all your mind, with all your soul, and with all your strength.

Invocation

The invocation is a prayer that aims at directing the worshipers' attention to God and communicating to God the intentions of the congregants to worship him. The invocation alerts worshipers of God's presence through the mood and commitment of prayer. In an invocation we call upon God to be present to us. Actually, this is the purpose of all prayer, isn't it? We call upon God to be God for us, as he has promised to be—God with us. In essence, whatever we pray for we are praying for God to come to us. The invocation often expresses this more explicitly than any other prayer. Several invocations are included to illustrate.

(1) Merciful and Holy Father, dwell in our midst. Make your abiding presence known to us. Come into your temple, our lives, and instruct us in our worship of you. In Christ's name we pray. Amen.

(2) Awaken us to your presence, Lord.

May our ultimate concern be our worship of you.

May our expanded concern include the whole world.

May our civic concern demonstrate responsible citizenship.

May our shared concern reveal that we are members of the body of Christ.

May our intimate concern communicate your love in our families.

Awaken us to your presence, Lord, today and every day. Amen.

(3) Father,
Great is your faithfulness, and we adore you.
Your presence is both comforting and frightening. We want to be confronted by your presence because we know that we are only truly ourselves when we are united with you. Be near to us today, Father. Amen.

(4) Disturb us with your presence, Lord.
    Nudge us out of our random thinking;
    Stir our lives with new compassion;
    Enlarge our vision with care;
    Broaden our service with love;
    Deepen our understanding with peace;
    Permeate our lives with hope.
    Disturb us with your presence, Lord. Amen.

(5)   God, our great liberator, set us free from the restraints which captivate us. Unlock our closed minds. Pry us loose from our prejudices. Untie our harbored resentments.
May our minds be opened doors through which your presence comes.
May our arms unfold and welcome all people to join with us in worship of you.
May our bitterness be melted into forgiveness, as you forgive us and free us from all our misbehavior. Amen.

Offertory Prayer

Our money is a symbol of our earnings and represents the fruit of our labor. We would not have labor were it not for the grace of God. Therefore, we could not have fruit for labor without labor. An offering is the tangible deposit from our labors that we can give regularly to the service of God through the church. The offering is a way of giving ourselves to God, and it symbolizes our personal commitment to God.

An offertory sentence or prayer is given before or after the offering is received to declare that what we do in giving is not simply a financial transaction, but a service to God. The offertory sentence or prayer focuses attention on the Giver of all gifts and is a collective expression of gratitude.

(1) Father, we come now to give our money. Our money symbolizes the abilities you have given us to work. Our use of money signifies the kind of stewards we are with what we have been entrusted. May our giving reveal our ultimate devotion to you and may our worship of you be enriched by the attitude with which we give. Amen.

(2) Lord, we claim to be followers of your Son in devotion and worship of you. May the attitude with which we give our offerings demonstrate the depth of our devotion and the height of our worship. May we always give you the first and the best of what we have to symbolize that we devote all that we are and have to you. Amen.

Pastoral Prayer

This prayer never is to be a presentation of the pastor's soul; rather, the pastoral prayer attempts to gather the needs of the congregation and to relate those needs to the terms of the truth of the Christian gospel and to current conditions. Perhaps this prayer would be identified better as the congregational prayer. This is the one prayer in the context of public worship that may be rounded out in all dimensions of prayer—adoration, thanksgiving, confession, petition, intercession, and dedication. This prayer, as all other prayers, must never be done for its beauty; rather its aim is to draw out from the congregation thoughtful worship and Christian dedication that must be given only to God. The world of nature, current events, and other situations may contribute to our awareness of God and be reflected in the pastoral prayer. Several examples follow to illustrate this type of prayer.

(1)   Almighty God and merciful Father, your bountiful care for us continually evokes praise and thanksgiving from our lives. Your love for us pricks our consciences and creates awareness of our dependence on you. Thank you for loving us and caring for us even when we have been unloving and uncaring.

Father, we confess to you that we have not loved our neighbors as ourselves because we have not loved ourselves. We have done many things that show hatred for ourselves. We overwork our minds and bodies and damage ourselves with undue pressure. We take things into our bodies excessively that destroy the health and vitality of our lives. Then when a product is taken off the market we scream loudly because of the inconvenience it is causing us. Lord, much of what we do and what we consume proclaims that we do not love ourselves.

We do not love our neighbors either. We don't even know them. We do not take the time to find out who a person is, much less what needs he has that we may help him meet. Father, how much good have we ever done for someone who disliked us or hated us? We know the answer, Lord. It is painful to admit that we have wronged so many. Father, we cry for mercy and forgiveness for ourselves, but when others ask the same of us we become cold, indifferent, and merciless. O Lord, great is our sin, but even greater is your grace and forgiveness. Please forgive us our trespasses and help us to forgive those who trespass against us.

Lord, multiple are the needs of others. Families of husbands and fathers who are missing in Vietnam had their hopes rekindled this week. How miserable such prolonged grief caused by separation must be! The effects of war remain ever with us. Father, people everywhere are clamoring to be treated as persons. Family members often treat each other as less than human. People of different races treat each other differently because of skin pigmentation. People of different nations treat each other differently because of their language differences. Father, the needs of people often are overwhelming. Help us, Father, to be part of the solution rather than part of the problem.

Lord, help us to renew our promises to you and to keep the promises we make. We give ourselves to you as instruments through whom you can speak and minister. In the name of Christ, our Lord, we pray. Amen.

(2)   Lord, we revere and adore you because your love to us is

boundless. The only binding you offer us is that which will bring healing to our wounded needs.

Thank you, Father, for unveiling yourself so completely in Jesus of Nazareth. Thank you for the glimpses of light we see as we look into the lives of others and see the illumination of your presence with them.

Father, we cannot count the times we have diminished your light in our lives. We have covered your light through our denials of you. You have called us to be the light of the world and we often choose darkness rather than light. We continue to want to draw attention to ourselves rather than to offer our lives as a means to point others to you. Your light brings order to our chaos but too often we choose to be obstructors of your light. Forgive us for such foolishness.

Lord, there are many who would like to receive your light today because your light brings life and order. We pray for those who do not experience the basic human rights we take for granted. We pray for those who do not have the nourishing food that our scraps contain. We pray for those who need the comfort of your presence in a time of pain, illness, and loss. May they feel the warmth of your light shining in their lives today.

Now, Father, help us to renew our commitments to you. We offer our lives to you, to be receptive to your guidance that we might become the light of the world which you have invited us to become. In the name of the Light of the world we pray. Amen.

(3) Father,

We are relational creatures by nature and by need. You have created us with the ability to relate to you and to relate to fellow human beings. Our nature drives us to you and to others and also often repels us from you and from others. Because it is out of our need to relate that we often struggle so much with who we are and where we are, it is out of our need to receive your acceptance and love that we often find ourselves trying to do all kinds of things to persuade you to love us.

Someway, somehow, we cannot seem to get it through our lives that you already love us. Someway, somehow, we cannot get it into our lives that were it all dependent upon what we could do to get you to love us, it would never come to pass.

Father, we are the same way in relationship to one another. We spend much of our energy and efforts trying to get others to like us, and to love us, and then, once in a while we are surprised, surprised that there are people who do like us and love us in spite of ourselves. In that moment of surprise, we get a clear glimpse of you.

Father, there are many needs represented in this sanctuary this morning. The needs of family members and friends who are struggling with illnesses, the needs of people here who have concerns that they are afraid to name, the needs of those here who are struggling with unknown factors in their lives.

There are needs beyond this sanctuary, needs of our world. We are concerned this morning, Father, for the Lebanese, for what is happening to them, what is being done to them. We are concerned for the Israelis and for what is happening to them and what is causing them to do what they do. We are troubled by the struggle and difficulty in South Yemen and the impact that it is having on the lives of people. Father, may your presence be made known to people in those places as well as here. May your love and care reach out to them and may they be receptive to your reaching to them, and may we, Father, be sensitive to your presence and seek to make peace in our relationship to you and our relationship to one another, for you have told us over and over again that only as we seek to make peace with one another and with you can we really experience peace beyond understanding. Grant us that kind of peace today and every day. In Christ's name we pray. Amen.

(4) Father,
Many of us have not even given you a passing thought this morning, much less sought to communicate with you. It is so easy for us to shift our lives into the routine of the day and go through the motions. Forgive us, Father.

We come here today, Father, out of different experiences, out of different needs and struggles. Some of us have lost jobs this week or have learned about the jobs we are going to lose, and so we struggle with that change in our lives. We feel very uneasy and insecure. Some of us have lost family members this week, some by death, some by changes in the family structure, some by changes in growth and development, some by changes in decisions that have been made, but all the changes have turned our lives upside down and we are in turmoil. We need the calm, settling, comforting awareness of your presence. We need your help and direction that we might take the long look at life, that we might in the midst of this time of worship draw strength from you and through our encounter with you offer ourselves as living gifts to you.

We are here this morning aware that we have put ourselves in a place where we may be confronted with our sins. We know that we need your confrontation. Even in the midst of our struggle and stress with that confrontation we are aware that in this place we also encounter your comfort, that we hear your forgiving word, and that we receive your bountiful grace. Help us, Father, as we are confronted with our sins and comforted by your forgiveness to also hear your call to be the persons you need and want us to be in this place at this time. In Christ's name we pray. Amen.

(5)   Father,
We are grateful to you for loving us and bringing us together in this place to worship. The beauty of the day reminds us of the beauty of your presence. The day itself is a part of your creation. We come to you at this time to worship you with all that we have and all that we are. And truly a part of our worshiping you is to see you more clearly, to love you more dearly, and to follow you more nearly. Father, may every aspect of our lives communicate that desire and intention.

Each of us comes also, Father, with her own agenda, with her specific and particular needs and concerns, each with her own troubles, each with her own checklist of needs. We offer them to you for your help, for your guidance, for your support. We ask for your instruction that you would protect us from clinging so tightly to our own agendas that we can't see yours. Forgive us for harboring our own checklist of needs so closely that we cannot see the needs of others. Enable us to discover that the needs we have are such as is common to those around us, and may we together commit ourselves to being a community of faith, supporting each other, encouraging each other, desiring to be church to one another.

May our worship of you in this hour reveal and reflect that kind of commitment. May we truly be the community of faith you need and want us to be in this place. In Christ's name we pray. Amen.

(6)   Father,

We are very grateful to you for calling us to be your people, for promising to be our God if we would be your people, promising to guide us and instruct us, promising to give us help and hope, courage and confidence through the journey of life.

Our experiences in life have shown us that there is a lot about our lives that is similar to the sailing excursion that Luke encountered. We find ourselves being blown and tossed about. We seek some type of safe harbor. We search for some kind of sheltered coast by which we may journey safely and securely.

We discover almost daily in the midst of the storms that life provides for us that you are our safe harbor, that you are the secure coast by which we may sail.

Help us, Father, each day to tie our lives to yours that we might journey into and through the storms of life, confident of your presence and care for us, assured of your presence and direction.

Often, Father, it is in the midst of public worship like this that we become sensitive to the wrongs we have committed. Sometimes it is the phrase of a hymn, the words of Scripture, a comment by a friend that stabs our lives into the awareness of our sins.

We confess our sins to you, Father. They are many. Legion have been the ways that we have turned against you this week. Multiple have been the statements that have not communicated your love and mercy. We beg your forgiveness. As we encounter your forgiveness, may we feel and sense the cleansing that is occurring in our lives, washing us, making us new and whole again.

And now that we feel and sense that cleansing, we find ourselves more able and willing to pray for others. We desire that you would hear our prayers in behalf of others. We know some of their needs. We are personally involved with some of them. We sense the needs of the world in which we live, the world of which you have made us stewards. We pray for the leaders of nations around the globe, and we pray for ourselves as citizens that we would be kept sensitive to the needs and rights of others. We ask that you would renew our relationship with you today, that this week of living might be a week of dedicated service to you because we have drawn strength from our worship of you. In the name of Christ Jesus, our Lord, we pray. Amen.

(7)   Father,

Many of us are in a summer slump. We haven't made a hit at anything we have tried lately. Some are eagerly awaiting vacation, anticipating the relaxation, rest, and refreshment it promises to bring. Others have had a vacation, or it had them. Somehow the vacation did not bring all that was expected of it. Be present to us, Father, and help us to deal with our disappointments.

Some of us are in a summer slump because we thought the change in routines would help us get away from some of our struggles. What we failed to see or refused to think about was that our troubles wouldn't go away just because we did. Enable us to draw strength from your presence, Father, to face our troubles and to seek realistic resolutions as we face them.

Sometimes, Father, we sense a slump in our relationships. Others seem disinterested in us, we feel rejected. Somehow our relationship to you is not what we think it ought to be or should be. At times we don't like who we are. Often we find someone else to blame. Often we are not very good company for others to keep. Our mood swings are radical and erratic. We need your stabilizing influence in our relationships with others and in our relationship with you. That is much of the reason why we are here this morning, seeking to draw strength and encouragement from you. Renew our lives, Father. Draw us out of the slumps into which we have gotten ourselves. Forgive us for trying to solve all of our problems all by ourselves. Renew our confidence and trust in you. In the name of Christ Jesus who taught us and teaches us to trust in you, we offer our prayer. Amen.

(8)   Father,
We come to you with our collected and collective needs. We have collected needs all week, needs which we have not voiced because we were too busy, because we were too frightened, because we were uncertain of your response, because we were unaware of our needs. Now in a place and time of worship our collected needs have become burdensome. Unburden us, Father. We have sinned against you and against one another through false testimony. We have manipulated others to get our way. We have held up double standards, one set for others and quite a different set for ourselves. Unburden us, Father, through your forgiveness. Take care of our collected needs and remove them from us.
We have collective needs, Father. We need your guidance and help to be a community of faith. We need your nudging to tear down our exclusive walls. We need your help to become inclusive people. We need to be Christ to each other within this congregation. We need to be Christ to each other in communities where we live and work. With your help we can be the salt of the earth and the light of the world. May it be so. May we collectively be the salt the earth needs and the light that the world needs to see. May it be so, Father, and may it begin in us, now. Amen.

(9)   Our Father, our Creator and Redeemer, we offer thanks to you for hearing our private and individual prayers. Thank you for hearing from our perspectives, for the expressions that we have made that also express something of our individuality. We also

have common needs—needs that affect all of us corporately. And we come now to offer those needs to you and to ask for your presence, for your direction, and for your help.

First of all, we all need forgiveness, for all of us have sinned against you. We confess our sins to you, realizing that it is important that we understand how to forgive and to be willing to forgive in order to experience forgiveness. So we ask from you forgiveness for our sins: for the unkind words we have spoken, for the belligerent attitudes we have portrayed, for the hostile stances we have taken, for the uncompromising approaches we have held out to others, for the insistence on things being done our way rather than your way, for the petty larceny we have committed by taking from others what is not ours to take. Hear our prayers of confession, Father. Cleanse us and clear us.

Hear our prayers, O Father, on behalf of others. We are concerned for them and their needs. For those who have physical ailments of which we are aware, we offer our prayers. For those who make decisions that affect our lives and the lives of people around the world, we pray that they will be sensitive to your kind of understanding and mercy—to your kind of peace and justice. And may that understanding temper their words, their attitudes, and their actions.

Now, O Father, renew a right spirit within us. Renew our covenant agreement with you. Remold us and remake us as your servants. In the name of Christ Jesus, our Lord, we offer our prayers. Amen.

(10) Father, as the gentle rain soaks the earth, may we be soaked in the gentle messages of love you constantly are beaming to us. As new life bursts forth from well-prepared and well-watered soil, may we be well nourished so that new life may burst forth in us and through us. We know that sin scorches our lives and makes them barren. We know that your forgiveness is the only oasis for our dry and parched lives. O Father, hear our confessions of sins. We have done wrong, but we have blamed it

on another. Forgive us. We have benefited from the hurt done to another and enjoyed it. Forgive us. We have passed on information that was entrusted to us. Forgive us. We have refused to look into the eyes of the hungry. Forgive us. We have resisted taking the hand of the lonely. Forgive us, Father. We have refused to touch the sick. Father, forgive us. We have avoided the bereaved and dying. O Lord, forgive us. Create clean hearts in us, Father. Restore us, remake us, remold us as your children. As you forgive us, as you remake us, may our lives be nourished by your presence.

May our lives be prepared to be your servants, and may new life burst forth in us and through us, O Lord, our God, our Creator and Redeemer and Sustainer. Amen.

Benedictions

The term *benediction* means "well-speaking" and is a prayer aimed at confirming the decisions, inspiration, and instruction that have occurred in worship, hoping that we may carry them out from the sanctuary into the ordinary days and common tasks of the week. Four examples are included.

(1)   The Lord is our strength. He is the provider of peace that passes understanding. Our trust in him has brought us this far. May we continue to trust in him and find him to be a faithful and encouraging friend through each day of this week. Amen.

(2)   Now may the God who invited us here, who has sustained us in our worship of him, who has forgiven us our sins, and who has renewed his covenant with us direct our living in our homes and offices in the days ahead. Amen.

(3)   Be assured as you leave this place that the God you worshiped here will be with you every day. He will go before you, directing your journey; he will be beneath you, giving you strength; he will be behind you protecting you; and he will be above you, creating the new you he is inviting you to be. Go with

this God who surrounds you. Amen.

(4)   Go now from the holy place into the marketplace. As you go, may the hope of God go before you, may the peace of God follow you, may the love of God undergird you, and may the joy of God hover over you. Amen.

Prayers for Special Occasions

Throughout the year there are special days and seasons of worship as well as special events in the lives of congregants that contribute to the significance of public worship. It is natural for prayers to reflect the importance of these special events. Following are prayers for a variety of special occasions.

Christian Home Emphasis. Father, we are gathered as part of your family. We come with multiple needs and a variety of gifts. We need your help to meet our needs and to distribute our gifts.

Some of us are singles. We are family. We struggle with aloneness, prejudice, and fear. We need support, understanding, and love.

Some of us are spouses. We grapple with our differences and are frustrated when our communication system collapses. We need space in our togetherness and togetherness in our space.

Some of us are grandparents. We have time, energy, and experience to invest. We want to give but not intrude. We want to receive but not demand. We need acceptance, affirmation, and sensitivity.

Some of us are teenagers. We are discovering who we are. We are wrestling with the powerful forces of sexuality and death. We need space, a place, and a face with a smile where the message of love is read.

Some of us are parents. We are overwhelmed by our responsibilities and troubled by our lack of skills. We need resources, education, empathy, and patience.

We are family. We argue. We are silent. We agree. We disagree. We get mad. We get glad. We share. We hoard. We hate. We love. We need support, encouragement, understanding, sensitivity, help, faith, hope, and love. Help us as family to be family to each other and to open our arms, hearts, and minds to embrace others in our family. May your family, Father, be our family. Amen.

Parent-Baby Dedication. Our Father, we thank you for the hands and hearts of the mothers and fathers who birthed and sustained Tom and Joan out of helplessness into dependency on you. May the influence of grandparents contribute to Annette's growth and maturity. May grandmother's house be a place of refuge for her when she thinks mom and dad do not understand. Thank you, Father, for Annette's grandparents.

Father, you open your hand and supply the real needs of every creature. We pray for your guidance and care which outdistances all our abilities to provide for ourselves. Give Tom and Joan work that will fulfill your purpose in their lives and help them provide food, shelter, clothing, and the beautiful things of life for their family. Steady their confidence when they are uncertain and give them companionship when decisions have to be made.

Thank you, Father, that Tom and Joan have been partners with each other and with you in creating and giving birth to a child. Grant them the grace to strengthen each other and Annette with love. May they continue to have access to each other's support through the power of your presence. May Tom and Joan relate to Annette with both strength and tenderness as they balance the power of love and insight.

Thank you, Father, for the gift of life you have wrapped in Annette. She is yours. We have the privilege of knowing her and sharing life with her. In dedicating her to you, we dedicate ourselves because Tom and Joan and the church have knitted spirit to spirit with hers in the larger family of humankind. We pray that strength of personality and length of days may be hers to realize. Protect Annette from war, hunger, and rejection, but teach her the mystery of suffering.

Grant us your grace, mercy, and peace as we join Annette in her pilgrimage. We pray through Jesus Christ, who is the pioneer of our faith. Amen.

Baptism. Thank you, Lord, for inviting us to be your children.

Thank you for the warmth we feel from you as we accept your love.

As we participate with Greg in his baptism, we are reliving our own. We are thankful for this outward, visible expression that portrays what is occurring inwardly and invisibly. Thank you for Greg's faith in Jesus Christ as Savior and Lord. Thank you that Greg wants to be a part of the body of Christ. We celebrate the joy of Greg's salvation and ours. We join our lives with his, Father. His joys and sorrows become ours. May we do the work of Christ together compassionately and courageously.

Father, guide Greg and us as we bury the past and rise to the present to love and serve you and one another. May Greg's baptism serve as a renewal of our commitment to be your ministers. In the name of the one who taught us to faith it, we pray. Amen.

The Lord's Supper. Father, as we prepare to partake of the Lord's Supper we are awed and troubled. When we consider how far you have come to love us, we are overwhelmed. The bread and cup represent the ultimate in giving for our benefit. Thank you, Father, for loving us so dearly and for going unlimited distance to communicate your love.

Father, partaking of the Supper is troubling for us. To take the contents of this loaf and this cup into our bodies is to commit ourselves to pour out our lives in commmunicating your love for all people. Partaking together of the Lord's Supper says that we all are part of the body of Christ. We are proclaiming more than we practice.

Help us, Father, to renew our covenant with you now. As we partake of the elements may we practice communion in our relationships and may we daily grow toward being the body of Christ for you in our world. Amen.

Rite of Passage. A pivotal date for young people in our culture is the sixteenth birthday. It is valuable for the youth and the church to recognize this doorway that leads toward adulthood. Here is a litany of support for sixteen-year-olds.

Pastor: We acknowledge that to become sixteen is a significant milestone in our culture.

People: We celebrate with these who have arrived at this threshold.

Pastor: To be sixteen is a key that unlocks many doors.

People: There is a mixture of freedom and responsibility behind those doors.

Pastor: We celebrate with you in this new freedom.

People: And we call you to meet the challenge of being a responsible person with your life; what you do with it, what you take into your life, and what comes out of your life.

Pastor: And we offer our prayers for you as the world opens before you.

People: We offer our support to undergird you as you launch out into the exciting unknown.

Pastor: May the love of God and our love bring you peace, encouragement, and support as you journey into a portion of life that has greater freedom and expanded responsibility.

People: Let it be so. Amen.

Religious Liberty. O Father, on this day which commemorates our national independence, make us ever mindful of our dependence on you. We use many of the same words to describe our country that we have used to describe you. Protect us from the idolatry of nation worship. Forgive us, Father, for the times when we have worshiped our country instead of you. Forgive us for our ignorance and arrogance that have kept us from knowing the difference. Keep us always aware that you are our Redeemer, not we ourselves. Make us ever mindful that you made us, not we ourselves. Help us, O Lord, to know that it is much more important to be cross-bearing Christians than flag-waving Americans; and whenever a choice between the two must be made, help us to know which is the right choice.

Father, we profess to believe that each person is unique and therefore different than we. We claim to believe that the body of

Christ is composed of many diverse members, as diverse as hands and ears and eyes are to each other. Yet when we get right down to it, we cluster ourselves with those who look and talk and smell the most like us. Then we expect others to become like us in order to be in our group. Forgive us, Father, for our exclusiveness. Enlarge our vision, Lord.

We who claim to be followers of the Way are citizens of your kingdom. Help our citizenship in your kingdom to inform our citizenship in the world. May we be protected both from narrow nationalism and from rigid conventionalism. May our living be informed by the living Christ who in word and deed reached out to all people everywhere as his brothers and sisters. May our citizenship be as inclusive as his. May our love be as unconditional as his. May our acceptance of others be as broad as his. May our mercy be as extensive as his. May our justice be as fair as his. May our forgiveness run as deep as his. Maybe then, Father, we can claim to be Christian citizens. May the needs and rights of all people be our concern. May the words we speak and the deeds we do at home, at work, at play, at church, convey our convictions that all people are our neighbors and that as citizens we have responsibility to all of them.

Thank you, Father, for setting us free through your redeeming love. May we be your liberators in the world so that justice may roll down like a river, mercy like an everflowing stream, and peace which outdistances our minds may permeate our lives.

We seek to offer this prayer like the one who brought us authentic liberty, Jesus Christ our Lord. Amen.

Christmas Eve. O Father, what a glorious, holy night this is. A night for kings and peasants, shepherds and angels, adults and children, wise men and fools—all their homage bring to the newborn King.

What a night! Even when our lives are in the shadows of despair, this night represents a glimmer of hope. Thank you, God, for breaking into our world.

What a night! Father, even the Scrooges of the world have

difficulty staying in character tonight. When you wrap your love in a human being, Father, it's nearly impossible to resist!

What a night! There are tensions and disturbances everywhere, yet there also is peace and calmness that goes beyond our understanding. Lord, it's your peace, isn't it? It calls us to reshape our lives because there is a better way to live!

What a night! Floods of joy fill our lives, Father. How can we respond to you this night but with great joy?

What a glorious, holy night this is, Father! It is the brightest night of the year because we are more conscious of the Light of the world tonight than any other night. Thank you, Father, for the Babe of Bethlehem who became the Man of Galilee to light the path of life for us. May we be the light of the world as Jesus said we are to be, and may our light begin shining tonight on this glorious, holy night. Amen.

Palm Sunday. Father, this is a peculiar day at the beginning of an uncomfortable week. I wonder what went through Jesus' mind on this day twenty centuries ago. The mood was celebrative. The crowd was electric. Did Jesus think that people finally were understanding? Or was his sudden popularity clear evidence to Jesus that the people had neither heard nor seen? What an emotional roller coaster Jesus must have ridden that week. To go from high acclaim to betrayal, denial, and death in five days is wrenching, blood-sweating agony.

Father, I wonder if this day and this week are really any different from any other days and weeks. Do we not applaud your presence with loud hosannas every Sunday and then betray, deny, and crucify you before Friday has passed? O merciful Father, forgive us. Forgive us for our piosity, hypocrisy, and religiosity. We make such a sham of your love. Forgive us.

O divine Master, may our pilgrimage through this particular day and this uncomfortable week serve as both a mirror and a window so that we may see ourselves more honestly and see you more clearly. May our renewed vision enable us to follow you more nearly and serve you more dearly. Amen.

Good Friday. Leader: We come together to remember the tragedy of our Lord's death.

Congregation: And to mourn what we do when we have God in our hands.

Leader: We remember Christ in the silence

Congregation: Of the cross.

Leader: We remember our brokenness

Congregation: And the cross.

Leader: We remember our loneliness

Congregation: And the cross.

Leader: We remember our commitment

Congregation: And the cross.

Leader: We come together to remember the tragedy of our Lord's death,

Congregation: And to mourn what we do when we have God in our hands.

Easter. Father, we are overwhelmed in the presence of your power. To restore life is something we are becoming able to do, but to resurrect one into continued living beyond this life is something only you have the power to do. Awareness of such power is awe-full for us.

Lord, we know that not only is resurrection a possibility for the future but also it is an existential reality now. But we cannot experience resurrection until we have confessed our sins to you. Numerous are our sins. Hear our confessions, O Lord, and deliver us from the death of sin to the resurrection of life. We have attempted to deal with our own sin through projection and repression. Deliver us, O Lord, through self-denial. In our closed-mindedness we have refused to be teachable. Deliver us, O Lord, through humility. Too often we have yielded to the temptation of dealing only with ourselves and never getting beyond ourselves. Deliver us, O Lord, through sharing. How often, Lord, we have functioned on the basis of superficial religion! Deliver us, O Lord, through understanding. We, too, have been the tragic figures of Judas and Peter. Deliver us, O Lord, through the abundant life you offer. Forgive us our sins and cleanse us from all unrighteousness.

All of us have gotten up out of sleep today and in so doing we have experienced in a symbolic way what it means to rise to new life as we have come to experience and enjoy a new day. The sunlight and breezes of this day have given us a glimpse of what it means for you to dwell in our lives and to raise us from deadness. May this day be for our lives like a new moon rising, like the sun bursting forth on a frost-covered morning. Father, may every poetic and prosaic verse within our beings burst forth and communicate our love and joy for your calling us to rise and follow you.

Merciful Father, comfort those in need today. The families of plane crash victims are overwhelmed by grief. Ease their sorrow. Those in Appalachia whose homes were washed away are stunned by their losses. Soothe their pain. The leaders of countries great and small have the destinies of the world's people in their hands. Steady their decisions that they might be reasonable, peaceful, and understanding. Our community has made strides in human relationships, but we have miles to go before we sleep. Guide us in leavening our community with your love and justice.

Now, Lord, we are eager and ready to renew our covenant with you. Come to us now, Lord, and resurrect us from our deadness into sensitive, alive persons. We offer our prayer in the name of the Resurrection and the Life. Amen.

Litany of Departure. Traditionally the church has had the responsibility of dealing with termination. The church both has taken this responsibility and had it thrust upon it. As a hospital chaplain, I observed a liver biopsy surgical procedure. The surgeon pointed out the malignancy, stated that there was no cure in this situation, turned to me and said, "We'll turn him over to you guys now."

There are many death-like experiences in our lives. One which is increasingly common in our mobile society is the ending of relationships which occurs when one moves from a community. The church often has dealt no better with termination than any other group. Sometimes we have done worse. I think we could model saying good-bye with a prayer or litany for people who are moving to another community and leaving a congregation of which we are a part. We do a variety of things to welcome them but very little if anything is done to facilitate saying good-bye. Our development of saying good-bye in the church could aid people in appropriate good-byes in their individual lives. Here is a litany for use when someone is leaving the church.

Pastor: We are relational creatures by nature and by need. God comes to us through the lives of others. We enjoy our relationships with one another and we grieve when one of those relationships ends. These sojourners who stand before us are leaving our congregation this week. What do you want them to know?

Congregation: We love you. You have been fellow strugglers with us in the faith. You have invested your lives with ours, and we are richer because of you.

Pastor: What do you, sojourners, want us to know?

Sojourners: We, too, are richer because of you. We love you. We want you to remember us. We want to continue as a part of your prayers and shared concerns.

Congregation: We shall remember you with joy. Our thoughts and prayers go with you as you leave us. You are family to us, and we shall never forget you.

Sojourners: We shall never forget you. Our memories of you will inspire us to deepen our faith, and we will continue to be supportive of this community of faith.

All: Now, may the God who called us from separate places to this place, and who has journeyed with us as we have traveled the same path, go with us on our separate paths. We are grateful to God for our years together, for mutual support and mutual forgiveness. We say good-bye and pray that our

memories of each other will be vivid and joyful.
We depart assured of God's help and hope. Amen.

I have attempted in this chapter to illustrate that learning to pray for public worship can enrich the worship of God and instruct worshipers in learning to pray. As I prepare prayers for worship, I discover that the prayers prepare me for the public worship of God.

Note

1. George Buttrick, class lecture, Spring 1972, Louisville Presbyterian Seminary, Louisville, Kentucky.

7

Learning to Pray for the World

And he came to Nazareth, where he had been brought up; and he went to the synagogue, as his custom was, on the sabbath day. And he stood up to read; and there was given to him the book of the prophet Isaiah. He opened the book and found the place where it was written,
> "The Spirit of the Lord is upon me,
> because he has anointed me to preach
>   good news to the poor.
> He has sent me to proclaim release
>   to the captives
> and recovering of sight to the blind,
> to set at liberty those who are
>   oppressed,
> to proclaim the acceptable year of
>   the Lord" (Luke 4:16-19).

Then he showed me the river of the water of life, bright as crystal, flowing from the throne of God and of the Lamb through the middle of the street of the city; also, on either side of the river, the tree of life with its twelve kinds of fruit, yielding its fruit each month; and the leaves of the tree were for the healing of the nations (Rev. 22:1-2).

At an international student conference, a young woman gave her name and said, "My home is Singapore, just on the other side of the world from here." Doesn't her statement express how small the world has become? We now talk about going around the world like we used to talk about going around the corner. Astronauts orbit the earth in ninety minutes. What a change from Jules Verne's idea of "around the world in eighty days." "It's a small world" is a more profound statement than any of us imagine.

World View

Every person has a theology. The choice is not between a theology and no theology; rather, the choice is between good theology and bad theology. Atheism and agnosticism are theological stances, as are Judaism and Christianity. How a person views God impacts on the way he communes with God about the world. As he communes with God his view of God and the world are affected.

Every person has a world view. It may be either limited and provincial or expansive and cosmopolitan. Whatever a person's world view is, the good news of Christ pushes out the walls of one's world and causes him to be more inclusive. This good news pushed on Peter's world view until he discovered that nothing God had created was unclean, including the Gentile, Cornelius. Paul, after being confronted by this good news and wrestling with its implications, made the revolutionary statement that there is neither Jew nor Greek, neither slave nor free, neither male nor female, but that all are one in Christ Jesus. The world view a person has affects how she prays for the world. As she prays for the world, her world view is affected.

We could benefit by seeing the world from another perspective. An expanding world view will help us see that this is one world. I suggest a trip to the moon because of what Charles Duke, a member of the Apollo 16 crew, said of his experience. Colonel Duke is the person who drove the lunar buggy on the surface of the moon. He described his feelings as he emerged from the space module and took his first tentative steps through the dust of the lunar surface, experiencing the unusual sensation of weightlessness. He told how after a few minutes he began to get over, to some degree, the newness of this experience and to settle down to a serious examination of this strange environment. He said he looked up—as he talked he paused and repeated this statement— looked *up* at the earth and stood silent for a moment drinking in the wonder and being conscious of a flood of new feelings as he looked afar at our world. He said at first it seemed incongruous to look up at the earth. After all, we are accustomed to looking up at the moon. As he stood looking up at the earth and marveling at its beauty, he indicated that for some inexplicable reason he lifted his open hand upward toward the earth and suddenly realized that the palm of his hand completely blocked from his view the whole world. He stood there, almost spellbound, for a considerable time, allowing the power of this experience to work its way throughout his mind and emotions and soul. He said that, for the first time in his life, he began to understand the oneness, the wholeness, the singleness of the world; and he said, further, that from that moment on his perception of the world as a community has been dramatically and permanently altered. The possibility of war among those who populate a world so singular seemed somehow inconceivable. The possibility that people, God's children, could live together in this singular world community and not be able to reach each other, touch each other, and communicate with each other seemed indefensible.

Many factors influence and impact our lives. These factors affect why, how, when, and for what we pray. William Sloane Coffin said, "A liberal is a person who thinks other people need help, and a radical is one who knows we're all in trouble."[1] This kind of radicality causes many to see the need to pray for the world. I live and work ten miles from the heart of the nation's capital. National and world news are local news. My world consciousness is continually being raised through the events that transpire in the news stories. The rainbow community where I live and awareness of the Washington street people cause the problems of racism, hunger, and poverty to take on human faces. Then to read passages of Scripture like the one at the beginning of this chapter summon me to be specific about applying the good news to the needs of the people of the world. I become increasingly aware that this is one world under one God, and what happens to one person affects all persons. Martin Luther King, Jr., said it more profoundly. "All life is inter-related. We are all caught in an inescapable network of mutuality, tied into a single garment of destiny. Whatever affects one directly, affects all indirectly. We are made to live together because of the inter-related structure of reality."[2]

One of the most significant discoveries continually unfolding to me is that my needs, struggles, failures, and successes are very similar to those of other people. This awareness of the solidarity of the human condition causes me to empathize with the poor, the captives, the blind, and the oppressed. This consciousness raising also causes me to realize that I really do not comprehend the impact that poverty, hunger, unemployment, imprisonment, and war have on the lives of people. Only as I have looked into the eyes of a few of these people have I seen the hollowness, the desperation, and the deep yearning for help that causes me to cry out for them. Prayer puts us in touch with people who share our same concerns, values, dreams, and pains. Bonding occurs as we share our commonality in prayer.

On July 28, 1982, I attended a press conference held by diverse religious leaders in support of prayer but in opposition to the proposed constitutional amendment regarding prayer. A female rabbi, a Jewish girl, a Buddhist monk, a Piscataway Indian, a Black Muslim, and a Christian minister offered prayers to God. I was aware of the breadth of ideologies and views that were represented, but regardless of name, all were addressing God as they knew him. The theme of each prayer was inviting God's help for the one praying to be sensitive to others and to protect one from imposing one's views or convictions on others. I had a keen sense of the presence of God and of solidarity with each of these persons. Barriers came down, and we were at one with each other and with God. This is a microcosm of the world and what the world needs.

Surely one thing we can do is to pray for the world. When we pray for the world, a bonding with the hurt and hungry, the terrified and the terrorists, the helpless and the hopeless begins to occur. Neither they nor we can remain the same as we pray for them. The barriers begin to come down, and we discover ourselves crossing lines we never thought we would cross.

The following prayer illustrates how prayer may begin with personal awareness and often pivot as the one praying is turned from an inward, narrow vision to an outward, expanding view of some of the needs of the world.

Our Father,
   Words are inadequate symbols we use to communicate concepts, feelings, and perceptions that well up from deep within our beings. *Gratitude* is a word we use to represent our awareness that

all we are and hope to be is a result of your unmerited favor.

In the recent weeks of autumn, we have beheld the beauty of the earth. Such beauty has caused us to contemplate your beauty, which is behind and beyond earthly beauty. In recent days, we have had a glimpse of Saturn and paused to worship you, the Master Designer of this solar system and others. Just this morning, as we arose from the death we call sleep, we were awed by the function of our bodies and concluded that we are wonderfully made. Such discovery has caused us to search for the depth of our existence. We have discovered that our lives are gifts from you. We are your handiwork. Thus, the basis of our genuine gratitude is the awareness and confession that we are created in your image.

Father, we are wonderfully made. We thank you for good minds that help us grasp knowledge and find truth. We are grateful for free will that allows us to choose our own direction and enables us to discover that we are not ourselves apart from you. Thank you, Father, for imagination which enables us to dream and picture ideals. We are grateful for personality that causes us to flesh-out our dreams and ideals.

Father, keep us ever mindful that we are yours, that this is one world which you have made, and that we are partners together as your servants to bring health and healing to your world and to your people. May the causes for which we campaign be permeated with love, justice, and mercy. May we be committed to the priority of an integrated community—integrated culturally, socially, economically, religiously, and racially. May our corner of the world reflect the harmony, diversity, and unity that you dream for all your worlds. May the bonds that unify us always be stronger than the differences which threaten to divide us.

Our Father, we thank you for your unmerited favor so generously showered upon us. May the authenticity of our thanksgiving be demonstrated through thanksliving. Amen.

This empathy informs the prayers I offer to God. Not only do my concerns become the world's concerns but also the world's concerns become my concerns. As I begin praying for others, I discover that others are gathered into an ever-inclusive circle. A poem, "Outwitted," by Edwin Markham expresses it well:

> He drew a circle that shut me out—
> Heretic, rebel, a thing to flout.
> But Love and I had the wit to win:
> We drew a circle that took him in!

There is a sense in which prayer, whether private or public, when it gets beyond rote memory, empty phrases, and vain words, begins to thaw our loyalties. This begins to be evident in the racist who cannot be cruel to the black child who lives next door or the greedy person who discovers himself disturbed to action by the starving face of a street person he could not get past quickly enough. When God wraps the needs of the world in human flesh, it is difficult to resist. Once a person starts praying about these needs and these people, the resistance is reduced even more.

Here is a prayer that refers to two people who made significant contributions to tear down the dividing wall of racial prejudice in the county where I live. Expressing to God appreciation for and awareness of their contributions caused me to enlarge my vision and to pray for community needs of righteousness, mercy, and justice, which also are world needs.

Our Father, Lord of the universe, our Sustainer and Redeemer, accept our gratitude for your gifts of life and love to us. Thank you for calling us into partnership with you and with one another that we might collaborate in bringing your universe to fulfillment and completion.

Father, thank you for the contributions that Councilman Fischer and Chief Reeves have made toward the betterment of human-kind. Continue to encourage them and us in our endeavors to make the communities where we live oases of openness and acceptance in the deserts of antagonism and hatred.

Regardless of the strides that have been made in human

relationships, Father, we know we have missed the mark of your intentions for us. We confess that we have hugged our prejudices and have locked ourselves behind doors of fear. We confess that as long as justice is realized for us, we have little concern about justice for all. Much of our work for justice for all has been tempered more with prejudice against those who are prejudiced than being tempered with mercy and kindness and righteousness for all.

But you, Father, are the God of us all. You want all of us to do justice, to love kindness, and to walk humbly with you. You are the drummer setting the cadence for our marching, and the cadence calls for justice to roll down like water and righteousness like an ever-flowing stream. No one is to be omitted in being treated justly and rightly. That is given in your gracious creativity in making us in your image.

May we with renewed sensitivity and expanded vigor increase our sphere of influence for justice and righteousness. May we evaluate this day and every day of living by asking ourselves if we have done justice, loved kindness, and walked humbly with you. These are the beats of a different drummer for some of us, but now more than ever we need to march to your cadence and make your cadence our own. May it be so in my life and in every life. Amen.

Often the statement, "I'll pray for you," is a glib phrase used to avoid relating to the person in need. However, when that phrase is spoken with authenticity, it will make a difference for the better in the pray-er's life, leading to constructive action on his part.

The problems of the world are monumental. Just the statistics related to world hunger are mind boggling. We often are immobilized by the monstrosity of the situation. In a "helpless" situation in his life, Jesus prayed, "Father, all things are possible with you." When we begin to pray about a concern we become more conscious of it and often with the consciousness comes some possible resolutions that begin to tear down the immobilizing wall of fear.

Managing the World

Uniquely, the world is in our hands, the hands of people around the globe. God is the owner of the universe, and he has done a very risky thing by choosing every human being to be a manager of part of the world for him. As far as the east is from the west is how far the hands of people join the hands of God in managing the universe. The grandiosity of managing the world occurs when one of us thinks he is capable of or has a mandate to manage it alone. The believability of managing the world occurs when we recognize our individual responsibility for being stewards of the corner of the world where we live and for lobbying for more meaningful living in our sphere of influence.

The problems and threats in the world are enormous. We are inundated with facts and figures about ecology and the hungry, the poor, the unemployed, and the diseased. None of our skills seem to match any of the needs. If they do, they wouldn't make a dent in the problems. We become immobilized. We cannot seem to find a place to begin and, thus, we do not start. The old Chinese proverb states that the journey of a thousand miles begins with a single step.

With regard to the magnitude of the needs of the world, what ought to be our first step? Prayer ought to be the first step. This is a simple but not a simplistic response. Throughout this book I have illustrated that prayer is an active, engaging, encountering dialogue with God. It is not a passive, uninvolved, throw-up-my-hands-can't-do-anything-else-so-I'll-mumble-a-few-"holy"-phrases-and-go-on-about-my-business monologue. We must learn to pray for the specific needs of the world. William Sloane Coffin complains, "There is too much dignity in too many prayers—dignity at the expense of specificity . . . So never mind how crude or how trivial your prayers may sound. There are no unimportant tears to God."[3]

Ecology

As managers of the world, our managerial responsibilities expand as the horizons of explorations and discovery in the world expand. Struggling with ecological and environmental issues has not been the forte of Western minds. The way we have dealt with diminishing resources is to move west.

Our throwaway mentality now is coming to haunt us. Two television commercials portray what this approach is doing to the world. In 1953 an advertisement sponsored by a beverage container company was seen on television. The commercial showed a person fishing, drinking from a can, tossing the can into the lake and saying, "Look how convenient these new cans are!" The second commercial appeared nearly twenty years later. It portrayed an American Indian looking out over a stream, a rusty metal can washed onto the shore at his feet, as a solitary tear trickled down his cheek.

Mass production and throwaway ethic support each other. World War II pushed mass production to unheard of levels and then we felt our economy depended on it. Madison Avenue was recruited to keep demand at artificially high levels. Whole new categories of "needs" were developed, such as the "need" for beer with gusto, the "need" for a bigger car, the "need" for two cars, the "need" for an economy car, and the "need" for designer jeans. Our economic system has become linear. At one end stands raw materials. We take them, manufacture them into products, and then throw away the residue and ultimately the products. Resources become waste.

We have been takers but not givers. We cannot forever take from creation and not give to it without bringing its utter collapse. Whose world is it? is a question for serious reflection. The answer shouted by our life-styles is that the world is ours for the taking and exploiting and destroying. The psalmist pondered this question and concluded,

> The earth is the Lord's and the fullness thereof,
> the world and those who dwell therein (24:1).

We have a responsibility to be managers, not manglers, of the world; we are to be its caretakers rather than its undertakers. In the book of beginnings, Genesis, the ancient storytellers point out the partnership between God and people. We have been put in charge of the world. We are the custodians of the earth and are to honor God by our caretaking of the earth.

Anyone who works with the soil knows, or soon learns, that he must put back into the soil what is being taken from it or the soil soon becomes useless. Those of us who are one or more generations removed from the farm may have difficulty comprehending this give and take regarding natural resources. The redemption of nature is related to the redemption of people, and the tragedy of nature and humankind are linked together. Personal salvation and cosmic redemption are inseparable. "For in him all the fulness of God was pleased to dwell, and through him to reconcile to himself all things, whether on earth or in heaven, making peace by the blood of his cross" (Col. 1:19-20).

It is wrong to destroy nature and add to its suffering. There is a moral and religious responsibility to conserve and care for nature's well-being. The love of neighbor and nature means to work for and to maintain an optimum ecological and environmental balance.

Hunger

My first awareness of world hunger came via television when I saw the pictures from Bangladesh of starving children with bloated stomachs. I was stunned and immobilized by what I saw. My first prayers for the hungry had no words. Actually I did not even recognize them as prayers at the time. Those pictures would not let me go, and I wonder now if it were love that would not let me go. My first verbal prayer response was, "This problem is so enormous. What can I do that would make a difference?" Of course, this rhetorical question in prayer was intended to be answered with "Nothing," and free me to go on to problems that I could solve. I was content with my "Nothing" answer. Perhaps it was the Spirit of God that continued to intercede for me, nudging me to open my eyes, my ears, and my life to the needs of hungry people. My prayer had the same words but with a different emphasis: "What can I do that would make a difference?"

The result of this prayer is that I have become more open to articles about hunger which help inform me about the problem of and possible solutions to hunger. I now get more regular exercise and eat less than any time in my life, and this is a direct result of my awareness of the hungry in the world. I am moving toward living more simply so that others may simply live. Starving millions and weight-watching millions exist in this global village. Prayer is a place for us to begin concerning hunger, praying for the hungry, and praying that we might be part of the solution rather than part of the problem. Through prayer a mission group in Oakhurst Baptist Church in Atlanta, Georgia, sought what they might do. Soon they were examining the hunger issue. They developed the periodical *Seeds*, encouraged that one Sunday each year be designated to inform about world hunger, and encouraged offerings for world hunger in Southern Bapist churches. Now millions of dollars are given each year specifically for world hunger. When you pray for those who are hungry, ask, What can I do that will make a difference? Such a prayer begins to put us in touch with those who are hungry. Once God gets us out of isolation, the possibilities are multiple. Here is a prayer about excess that may help raise our consciousness both about the environment and about the hungry.

Father,
Often we are warmed by being the light and salt of the earth. But the warmth turns icy cold when in honesty we become conscious of how far short we are of being who and what you have invited us to be.

We have lived excessively. We eat too much, we drink too much, and we work too much. Through our excesses, we have sinned against you, against others, and against ourselves. We have harmed our lives, your gifts to us. Forgive us. We have taken food from others by overconsuming ourselves. We suffer from unlimited wanting and equate wants with needs. Father, forgive us. At least once a year we open our eyes to those who do not have enough. Father, help us to do something about empty stomachs in January and July, as well as in November. We have too much while others have too little. May we be part of the solution to this problem, and may we begin now. Amen.

Homeless

Jesus said that foxes have holes and birds have nests, but the Son of man had nowhere to lay his head. I don't comprehend the impact of that statement because I always have had a place to go. Never have I been homeless. I see the homeless in my city, and I shudder in realizing that the street is home for them. Everything they own—consisting of the clothes they wear—is in plain view. Only a piece of newspaper is between them and the bitter winter cold. Sometime during the day they may make it to a soup kitchen for enough food to keep them existing for another day. At best, these street people are existing. I am shocked at what life is for them; and upon seeing them, often I am eager to return to the sanitized suburbs to keep myself "pure and holy and undefiled."

When I was in school, a teacher occasionally would tell us what questions would be on a final examination. I reacted with mixed feelings. I was relieved to know exactly what would be asked, but I also felt uneasy because I knew evidence of knowledge gained independently of class would be expected. In essence Jesus told us what would be required of us on the final examination of our living: "I was hungry and you gave me food. I was hungry and you gave me no food" (Matt. 25:35,42).

How we relate to other people, especially when they are in need, is the acid test of how we relate to Christ. These words of the final examination were not invented by the church. The church has never been comfortable with this stance. I have lots of company in my discomfort with the homeless and my desire to avoid them and to pretend I do not see them. There is no lasting comfort in knowing I have partners in my discomfort and in my detached approach to human need.

I seem compelled to pray for the homeless. Once again my loyalties thaw a little, as a result, and I begin identifying with them. This is a start toward reaching out to them.

Father,

I don't want to admit that John is a human being. I justify my distance if he is a statistic, just one of the millions who are homeless and helpless.

What happened to John, Lord? He's out of work, and no wonder. He is unclean and unkempt. Who would hire him? He doesn't want to work or he'd get a job. The paper is full of want ads every day. I can keep my smugness as long as John stays downtown and I stay in sanitary suburbia. But God, once I walk on John's street and look into his eyes, he won't go away. Those empty, hollow, haggard eyes won't leave me alone.

What happened to John, Lord? When he came as a child, we turned him away. He always sat in the back of the class at school, just on the fringe. He wasn't sure anyone would accept him, and we didn't. He was slow with the answers and so the teacher gave her attention to the quick children. We did, too, because we needed her approval to survive. We kept pushing John to the edge. When the jobs came, we ran past John, took the good ones for ourselves, and told John he could have what was left. Once we had him on the edge, we wanted to keep him there. We spat on him with ridicule and kicked him with contempt. We middle-of-the roaders need marginal people like John to help us be sure we are in the middle and not on the edge. Now John is about to fall off the edge. He is grasping for any morsel that we might drop.

O God, look at what we've done to your son. We're crucifying another one of your children. John condemns us. No, we have condemned ourselves. We see our condemnation in his eyes. That is where we hear you say, "It is I." God, forgive us! John's eyes have condemned us, and they have awakened us. Help us to go to the edge and pull John, and Mary, and Tom back into life. Amen.

Peace

The literature of civilization is filled with compositions expressing longings for peace. In those compositions, peace has various meanings: absence of war, serenity, restored relationship between God and humanity. For many of us, peace has a functional definition. Peace for us is the ability to pursue the ordinary routines we have defined for ourselves without interruption, stress, or struggle. When the boss complains or the children yell, we are heard begging, "Give me a little peace and quiet!"

Micah (4:1-7) and other biblical writers express what peace is. The biblical understanding of peace means the state of wholeness possessed by persons or groups. The characteristics of this wholeness include: health, prosperity, and security as a result of spiritual completeness of the covenant relationship with God. Some discount Micah's words as idealistic reference to a future age in another world, but Micah was speaking about his age and his words are applicable to our age. He believed that, when people learned from God, they would put down their swords and spears and take up plows and pruning knives to cultivate the earth and care for it as God intended.

There is no greater longing in Scripture than the longing for world peace. How much more intense this yearning is for many today. When the atomic bomb was developed, we moved into the nuclear age, and nothing has been so constant as the turbulent change which has occurred since 1945. The lack of wholeness runs the gamut of needs in my city. On one end of the spectrum are those who are homeless and those who have no idea when or if they will eat again. On the other end are those who have plenty to eat but who are gravely concerned about the annihilation of the entire human race.

Many wars rage and ravish human lives. The torrents of poverty, hunger, and disease either pound people into oblivion or render them helpless. People need peace from these wars, and I have previously illustrated the significance of praying for these.

With regard to war in its classical definition, the church has chosen one of three attitudes toward war: pacifism, the doctrine of the just war, and the crusade. Today our technology has outstripped our morality and our theology. We have moved to the crater's edge and are staring at the black night of our souls. We have the power not only to destroy every human being but also to cancel the numberless multitudes of unconceived people. Were a nuclear war to occur, the death of all people in the world and the death of the human species could happen simultaneously.

Maybe in no arena do we feel more helpless than in working for world peace. Perhaps your thinking is similar to mine.

I barely manage to cast one vote each November. I do not make the laws, and I do not enforce them. I am not a negotiator for peace with other nations. My views and opinions have not been solicited. What little thinking I allow myself to do about nuclear war causes me to shudder, to feel completely helpless, and to refuse to think about it anymore.

We suffer from what Robert Jay Lifton calls "psychic numbing."[4] Yet, no one predicted how many voices would begin to be raised against nuclear armaments. No one imagined that 500,000 demonstrators would gather at the United Nations in June 1982 in a peaceful peace demonstration. Where did this movement begin? It bubbled up in the church and now is flowing out into the world. It began with people praying, praying for the world and for themselves as managers of the world. Here is where we can begin. We can pray for peace in our relationships, and we can offer our energies to be used for peace throughout the world.

O God, our Creator, we are partners with you in creating the world as we know it today.

Never has your title, Creator, brought such condemnation upon us as it now does. We are the crown of your creation. We are your handiwork, which you announced was "very good." What manner of evil has brought us to the point where we can wipe out not only all of creation but also end the human enterprise altogether? We know that such power is demonic because we have no authority to use this destructive power. O God, forgive us for the demon that we have created.

Father, we are demon possessed by our clamor for security. We are permitting our fears to control us. We need to be depossessed. We know that authentic security rests with you and that your love casts out fear. Help us to trust you rather than ourselves and to allow your love to wash away our fears. Help us to diffuse our bombs and direct our energy and resources away from destructiveness and divisiveness toward human wholeness. Father, make us look into the faces of those we would destroy. Help us to see that we have made them our shadow sides. Make us know that to destroy them is to destroy ourselves. Convince us that they are your creation too. They have families and friends like we. They have dreams and ambitions like we. They have needs and hurts like we. They need us, and we need them. Father, protect us from destroying each other.

O God, our Sustainer, help us to be partners with you in sustaining the world. We are family, your family. Making peace begins with me, doesn't it, Lord? It begins with how I relate to those in my primary relationships. Help me to sow the seeds of peace rather than violence with my family and friends. Help me to develop these gifts of peacemaking: affirmation of others, respect for the differences of others, the challenge of cooperation, and creative resolution of conflict. Father, improve my peacemaking efforts at home. Sustain peace in your world by beginning with me.

O God, our Redeemer, instruct us in redemptive ways to resolve conflict. Enable us to love our enemies and to pray for those who persecute us. Forgive us for our desires and plans to destroy others. Permeate our lives with an attitude of forgiveness. Enable us to forgive without limit because we have been forgiven without limit. Guide us to create peace where there is hatred and reconciliation where there is separation.

Father, make us instruments of your peace. May our partnership with you as Creator, Sustainer, and Redeemer cause us to beat our destructive attitudes into constructive relationships. May we be makers of peace where we live and work and play. May your peace permeate the world and may it begin with me, today. Amen.

As our sensitivity to others increases, we become more aware of the wars that are raging in their lives. Unless they find some peace in their lives, they will project their raging onto others. In one sense, people always are living in troubled times. Here is a prayer for peace for people living in such unrest.

Father,

We are living in troubled times. Our lives are but brief interludes between birth and death, and these interludes are filled with pain and suffering. There seems to be no ease for us, there is no balm in Gilead for us. We hear proclamations of peace on earth, goodwill to men, but there are times when it seems there is no peace because hate is strong, and mocks the song of peace on earth, goodwill to men.

Every age has been the best of times and the worst of times, Father. We have more with which to cope—more tension, more broken relationships. We also have more resources—better technology, better medical attention, more freedom to find solutions. God, you are still attempting to come to us through one another and you want to come to others through us.

Father, you are the one force of stability who has been in all the ages and who has transcended all the ages. Your abiding presence has brought hope and peace beyond understanding throughout the centuries, and we believe you are seeking to come to us in hope and peace today.

Father, we know there are many near us who are not at peace. We see their unrest and feel their discomfort. Grant that we might be peacemakers in their lives and be a part of the solution to the tension that is destroying them. Come in peace for them through us, Father. Lord, just when we think life is in order for us, a crisis arises which disrupts our plans and intentions. Help us to know, Father, that you are seeking to come in peace to us today. Enable us to be receptive to your coming.

We offer our prayer in the name of the ultimate peacemaker, Jesus Christ, our Lord. Amen.

One of our greatest needs is for peace and justice to permeate our living. As these take root in our lives, we will not only pray for peace and justice but also practice them. Here is a prayer expressing the desire for peace and justice.

Almighty God,
    Grant us peace and justice for our time and all times. When peace and justice are not known in our minds, not felt in our hearts, and not at work in our hands and feet, bitterness and prejudice prevail, with oppression and injustice for all.
    May peace be more than a word; may it be our character. We

are a diverse people with a common belief in the holiness of the
earth and in the sanctity of all life, and with a common need to be
at peace with all people.

May we be makers of peace in our homes, in our communities,
and in the world.

May justice be more than a deed, may it be our motivation.

We affirm that our earth's security rests
    in the justice of adequate housing and food,
    in the justice of meaningful education and work,
    in the justice of economic order that gives
everyone access to the earth's abundance,
    in the justice of human relationships nourished
by cooperation rather than diminished by competition,
    in the justice of safe, clean, renewable energy.

May we be practitioners of justice in our work and in our leisure.

May we develop wisdom, courage, and strength that will enable
us to rise above special interest, party strife, and selfish nationalism to act out of concern for all humankind.

May our every word and deed cause justice to flow like a river
and mercy like a never ending stream. Amen.

Prayer puts us in touch with other people. As we pray for specific
persons and about definite world situations, we begin to develop a bond
with those people and their conditions. If we are serious about
intercessory prayer, then is not part of our reason for praying to place
part of our energy at God's disposal to use as he is able for those
persons and their conditions? Our learning to pray for the world
includes the troubles and conflicts which other nations experience.

O Divine Master,

Ours is a troubled generation living in a disturbed world. There
is trouble in the East. The leadership in China has changed and
the citizens feel insecurity and upheaval. May their transition be a
tranquil one.

There is trouble in the Middle East. We are grateful for the
cease-fire between Syria and Israel. We hope this temporary

agreement will become a permanent one. May the Arabs and Jews discover that they are more alike than different and may they work for their mutual benefit.

There is trouble in the South. We all have our Falklands, those people and places that won't do things our way and threaten our authority. May Britain and Argentina see the foolishness of their fighting and stop it today. Help them to discover their kinship and to respect each other.

We are appalled at the wholesale murders in Uganda. These tragedies are revolting to us. We do not understand. We pray for the victims and their families, and we pray for those who murdered for whatever cause. We cannot excuse their deeds, but we sense their terror and helplessness. Calm them, Father.

Lord, bring peace to Ireland. I wonder how many people have prayed for that and how many more have worked for peace there. Christians have more in common than our conflicts, but we cannot prove that in Ireland. God, I ache deep in my soul when I hear and see the bitterness and animosity hurled between Protestants and Catholics there. God, make them stop fighting and start constructive efforts toward the brotherhood and sisterhood of humanity.

The Soviet Union and the United States are at a pivotal point, Father. They can reduce global anxiety with disarmament talks and actions. We hold our hopes at bay because at times these leaders seem to want us to hate each other to keep the economies going. Father, cleanse us of our us-and-them mentality and enable us to work for the betterment of your creation everywhere. Protect us from projecting onto the Soviets the dark sides of ourselves.

Father, we feel there is trouble on every hand. Reassure us we are not without a Friend. Protect us from despair which could easily beset us. Make us to see that all is not lost and challenge us to be at peace with all people, beginning with our families and friends whom we see daily.

We offer our prayer like the Prince of Peace who teaches us to pray. Amen.

Decision Makers

The direction of nations and the destinies of people are determined by the decisions the national lawmakers and leaders make. Decision makers vary from democratic to autocratic to totalitarian. Many of us have no concept of the pressures these persons feel or the strain under which many of them work. Some of them at times are unaware of how heavy their task weighs upon their lives.

We need to pray for world decision makers because their loads are heavy, as are ours, because they are limited beings, as are we, because we need to better understand them, and because we are partners with them as managers of the world. Our prayers for them are not to baptize their actions but to guide them and us toward clearer thinking in making decisions that will benefit all people everywhere.

Our Father,

Many people will make decisions today that will affect our lives. They are power brokers in nations great and small, and they hold the destinies of the world's people in their hands. Steady their decisions so that they might be reasonable, peaceful, and understanding. We have made strides in human relationships, Father, but we have miles to go before we sleep. Guide all of us who make decisions to leaven the world with love and justice.

Thank you, Father, for persons throughout the world who are willing to be decision makers. We appreciate their willingness to be decision makers. We appreciate their willingness to expose themselves to the public eye and public scrutiny. The issues with which they must deal are mind boggling. Protect them from being overwhelmed by their nations' agendas and grant them the wisdom to deal sanely with the issues one at a time. Give them needed patience to work equitable compromises that will help meet the needs of people and offer them the necessary strength to struggle to find the best solutions for all people. Prevent them from giving in to the pressures of special interest groups, and do not let the serpent of personal advancement blind their wisdom and insight.

Father, we are grateful for the energy and enthusiasm that you generate in world decision makers to enable them to deal with tough issues. Do not permit them to become so power hungry that they fail to care for the hungry; do not let them bask in the warmth of popularity so long that they forget those who are cold and unpopular; do not let them become so enamored with their positions that they are out of touch with those who have no position; don't let them be seduced by might-makes-right schemes that always reduce people to pawns on a political chessboard.

As these decision makers go about their daily tasks, make them mindful of your presence and of your desire to be a partner with them in their decisions. May your love undergird them, may your joy hover over them, may your hope go before them, and may your peace permeate their lives and their relationships.

Thank you for hearing our prayer and attending to our concerns. Amen.

Racism

As our world view enlarges, the global village shrinks. I grew up in a semi-rural community that was White, Anglo-Saxon, Protestant, and Republican. I thought everyone in the world was just like the people in Monticello, Kentucky. Industrialization and mass media had their leveling effect on our community, as they did on other communities. The result was that we began to see the plurality of the world, as well as discover connectedness to parts of the globe we had not known existed prior to 1950.

Prior to 1954 issues were black and white; and that was how they usually were decided, in favor of white and against black. Issues began to have a great deal of gray, but people preferred to rely on emotions rather than to deal with conflictual issues. Decades after the Supreme Court ruling which called for school integration and more than one hundred years after emancipation, racism continues to be one of the major unresolved ethical issues in the United States, as well as in other parts of the world. Racism underlies much of the tension felt in our communities, as well as permeating our attitudes about other nations.

The good news has not touched every part of each of our lives. Our prejudices strain our credibility of being converted Christians. Each of us has some biases and prejudiced opinions. Often our prejudices come to consciousness in the midst of tension and uneasiness. Redemption from racism must begin with me, and prayer is an appropriate way to begin dealing with this issue.

Loving Creator,

We acknowledge that you are the Maker of heaven and earth and all that dwell therein. We cannot understand why different races cannot get along. We don't mind a few blacks or Koreans being around us until we are in the minority. Then we flee to some other community. We have to protect our property value, you know.

Father, we quickly blame the troubles of our time on the pigmentation of someone else's skin. Forgive us for our racism. We always are asking for a handout from you, Lord. Today we want to give you some things. We want to give you our tinted eyes that have seen only white. We want to give you our small hearts that will not include Hispanics. We want to give you our short arms that will not reach the Japanese. We want to give you our crooked hands that will not help blacks and browns. We want to give our little feet that never will walk in the Indian's moccasins.

Father, we do not want to be color blind; rather, we want to see your rainbow refracted in the skins of your people. May the multi-colors of our brothers and sisters be your sign of hope to our age.

We have some emotions we want to give you, Father. We give you our fear so there will be room for love. We give you our bitterness so there will be room for mercy. We give you our hatred so there will be room for justice.

Lord, help us tear down the walls of racism we have built. We have walled others out and ourselves in, and we are suffocating in our self-made prisons. Everyone is beautiful in his own way. Help us celebrate your beauty in the colorful lives who cross our paths, live in our communities, attend our schools, work at our jobs, and worship at our churches. Amen.

Isolationism

The more things have changed, the more we have attempted to remain the same. For many people, the transition from the farm to the city has been only a geographical move and not an emotional one. People remain detached from each other and hide behind their clamor for privacy. Bombarded through the media by events of destruction, violence, terrorism, and suffering, people become saturated by human need. Overwhelmed by so many needs, they become numb to the human cry for help and thus can pass by and do nothing while someone is attacked, robbed, or beaten. People feel threatened, insecure, and vulnerable. They are afraid to risk community. They withdraw into apartment complexes or lock themselves into the security of suburbia and come out only when absolutely necessary—to go to work and to get supplies.

The loneliest experience I have ever had occurred in the summer of 1968. I had a three-day layover in Trinidad on my way to Guyana, South America. I was traveling alone, which was difficult, but the loneliness was intensified because of a language barrier. Although English was the spoken language, the accent made it impossible for me to understand what was being said, but others could understand me. I began to feel intimidated, then frightened, and eventually stupid; the loneliness increased; I felt isolated even with people all around me. I was so overcome by fear that in the restaurant I would point to the items on the menu that I wanted rather than saying them, even though the menu was printed in English and the waiter understood my English. In my isolation, I regressed in my ability to communicate and negated any opportunity to relate to anyone.

People do not have to travel to other nations to experience isolation. A degree of isolation is felt when a person moves from one place to another, whether that be off to college, into a new community, a new job, or a move into the city. Add to this move the language and culture that are integrated parts of people whether they are from the other side of the tracks or the other side of the world, and the shocking effect is intense. A common protective maneuver is to isolate. We need to pray for the lonely people of the world as a start toward building community.

Father, we are all lonely people.

We are lonely because of the losses we have experienced, because of choices we have made, because of what has been done to us, because of what we have done.

Father, we are all lovely people.

We are lovely because you have made us and because you love us.

We need fellowship that is more than eating;

We need relationship that is more than speaking;

We need caring that is more than empty phrases;

We need to look at each other and see love looking back at us.

We need bridges of loveliness to cross over our loneliness.
Amen.

Technological advances contribute to global shrinkage and personal isolation which result in the loss of personhood. As this loss is multiplied millions of times the world over, people project similar fears and withdrawal onto classes and ethnics within their culture and onto other nations. The result is that when someone speaks of the Germans or the Russians, if any faces come to mind they are those of Hitler or Stalin or Breshnev or Andropov. More likely, no faces appear in our minds because we have run into isolation for refuge by projecting that there are no human beings out there, only beasts who will malign and destroy us. Isolation is a problem faced by world citizens, and we need to learn to pray for one another in the struggle against loneliness and isolation.

If people struggle as much in their attempts to pray for the world as I have struggled in attempting to write about praying for the world, then no wonder the world is in the condition it is. E. B. White has delineated clearly the issue for me.

If the world were merely seductive, that would be easy. If it were merely challenging that would be no problem, but I arise in the morning torn between a desire to improve (or save) the world and a desire to enjoy (or savor) the world. This makes it hard to plan the day.[5]

Since I began this chapter out in space, I may as well end it there too.

One who has been above the world expresses what our perspective of the world needs to be. Joseph Allen was one of the astronauts on the last precommercial flight of the space shuttle *Columbia*. He said that from space, as one looks at the earth, there are no distinctions of people by color, race, social, economic, or philosophical persuasion. It is all one entity.

Maybe none of us ever will have the opportunity to view the world from outer space; but as we learn to pray, we learn that the view of the world both from outer space and inner space is the same. There are no distinctions of people. The world is all one entity.

Learning to pray is an evolving process. It is a direction rather than a station. My prayer learning has been telescopic in nature, which is the design of this book. Being most conscious of my needs and inadequacies, I usually begin praying for myself; however, I cannot pray long before I become conscious of the needs of others, and praying begins to have social dimensions. *I* becomes *we* and *my* becomes *our*. The persons for whom I pray telescope to include friends and enemies, the sick, the grief-sufferers, the worshipers, and fellow human beings everywhere. I hope you will join me in this lifelong pilgrimage of learning to pray.

Notes

1. William Sloane Coffin, American Baptist Peace Conference, Washington, D.C., November 11, 1982.

2. Martin Luther King, Jr., quoted in Maynard Shelly, *New Call for Peacemakers* (Newton, Kansas: Faith & Life Press, 1979), p. 12.

3. William Sloane Coffin, *The Courage to Love* (New York: Harper & Row, 1982), p. 25.

4. David M. Alpern, "Who's Who in the Movement," *Newsweek*, April 26, 1982, pp. 22-23.

5. E. B. White, *International Herald Tribune*, July 13, 1968, p. 16.

Bibliography

Books

Buechner, Frederick. *Wishful Thinking*. New York: Harper and Row, 1973.

Coffin, William Sloane. *The Courage to Love*. New York: Harper and Row, 1982.

Crotwell, Helen Gray, ed. *Women and the Word*. Philadelphia: Fortress Press, 1978.

Elkind, David. "The Child's Conception of Prayer," *The Child's Reality: Three Developmental Themes*. Hillsdale, New Jersey, Laurence Erlbaum Associates, 1978.

Johnson, Paul E. *Psychology of Religion*. New York: Abingdon Press, 1959.

Schonberg, Bernard, ed. *Loss and Grief: Psychological Management in Medical Practice*. New York: W.W. Norton and Company, Inc., 1970.

Shelly, Maynard. *New Call for Peacemakers*. Newton, Kansas: Faith and Life Press, 1979.

Tillich, Paul. *The Courage to Be*. New Haven: Yale University Press, 1952.

Westberg, Granger. *Good Grief*. Philadelphia: Fortress Press, 1962.

Periodicals

Alpern, David M. "Who's Who in the Movement," *Newsweek*, Vol. XCIX, No. 17, April 26, 1982.

Capps, Donald. "The Psychology of Petitionary Prayer," *Theology Today*. Vol. XXXIX, No. 2.

Hendry, George S. "The Life Line of Theology," *The Princeton Seminary Bulletin 65*, 1972.

Jennings, Theodore W., Jr. "Prayer: The Call for God," *The Christian Century*, April 15, 1981.

Newcomb, Theodore. "Approach to the Study of Communication," *Psychological Review* 60, 1953.

White, E. B. *International Herald Tribune*, July 13, 1968.